Broken and Blessed

How God Used One Imperfect Family to Change the World

Jessica LaGrone

A Bible Study on Genesis

ABINGDON PRESS

Nashville

BROKEN AND BLESSED: HOW GOD USED ONE IMPERFECT
FAMILY TO CHANGE THE WORLD:
A BIBLE STUDY ON GENESIS

Copyright © 2014 Abingdon Press

This book is printed on acid-free paper.

ISBN 978-1-4267-7837-7

14 15 16 17 18 19 20 21 22 23—10 9 8 7 6 5 4 3 2 1
MANUFACTURED IN THE UNITED STATES OF AMERICA

Contents

Introduction

In college I signed up for "Sociology of the Family." We all groaned about these required liberal arts classes, since they had nothing to do with our majors. And, of course, we were sure our majors had everything to do with what we would do for the rest of our lives. Mine was pre-med biology. Go figure.

On the very first day of class our professor opened with a question: "Tell me about your family." I immediately felt uncomfortable. This was a new semester, a new school year. I was convinced that telling people about my family background was not the best way to make a good first impression. The fact is, somewhere during the explanation of my family history of divorce, remarriage, re-divorce, alcoholism, suicide, family secrets and family feuds, stepparents, stepcousins, stepgrandparents, stepdogs and stepcats, I often began to feel like I was telling more about the plot-line of a soap opera than my own family tree.

I looked around to see if I could sneak out for a bathroom break and conveniently miss my turn to share—or at least hide under my desk until the whole exercise was over. Then a surprising thing happened. The girl who went first introduced herself, took a deep breath, and said: "I didn't really grow up in a perfect family. My parents got divorced and remarried, but they only lived two streets apart, so we would spend one night at one house and one night at the other. It was a weird way to grow up."

The next guy said: "I don't really have a normal family either. My dad died when I was really young, and we moved in with my grandparents."

This scenario went on and on around the room. There was the guy who had more stepsiblings than the Brady Bunch, and the girl who had been adopted from another country and looked nothing like her parents. There was the girl who grew up in a military family and had moved around so much that she couldn't really say where she was from. Then there were people who had always felt different because they didn't have any brothers or sisters.

By the time my turn came, I was feeling more comfortable about my own family! The interesting thing was that most people prefaced their introduction by giving some sort of disclaimer that their family was "not perfect" or "not like everyone else's." It began to occur to me that there was no such thing as a normal family! In fact, all of our families were perfectly imperfect.

There is probably something that makes your family unlike everyone else's family. Some of those unique characteristics are wonderful things that we celebrate. Others make us feel, as I did that day in class, like there is something that makes us different in a not-so-wonderful way. What we sometimes forget is that because every family is different and distinctive, this actually gives all families something in common.

Nowhere is this truer than in the Book of Genesis. Genesis was one of my favorite books of the Bible long before I realized that all of the main characters in it are related. Genesis traces the branches of a single, perfectly imperfect family and God's constant and unfailing love for them.

The Book of Genesis serves as a kind of scrapbook for this family, recording both the good and the bad pictures of their experiences through the years. Some of their stories will make you smile with affection for these unusual kinfolk and their antics. Others may make you blush, cry, or shake your fist in anger. Part of the beauty of this family's story is that, while they are not perfect, they were chosen by God for a specific calling and purpose. They are both broken and blessed.

As I began to read the Genesis narrative as a family story, it helped me to understand that God doesn't wait for us to be perfect before loving us. I decided that if God chose to use this unusual family for His purposes, then maybe He wants to use me and my family to change the world too.

Something very personal happens when we flip forward in the Bible's family scrapbook to the New Testament. We find our own pictures there. Galatians promises us that because we belong to Christ, we are now part of the Genesis family, heirs to all the promises of blessing God made to Abraham and Sarah and their family long ago (Galatians 3:29). Now when we read Genesis, we can do so with the realization that this is our story, our family, and the origin of our own brokenness and blessing.

Maybe you sometimes feel as though your family came right out of a soap opera, like the characters and antics you find there could win the prize for putting the "fun" back in dysfunctional. If so, this study is for you.

Maybe you feel like you've had a uniquely normal family experience, nothing too far out of the ordinary. Maybe there are a few black sheep here and there in your family tree, but for the most part you are blessed by family who have loved you and given you a stable foundation to build on. If so, this study is for you.

Or maybe you consider yours to be the perfect family. Perhaps you're thinking, *There's not even a moderately gray sheep in my family, much less any black sheep.* If that's you, just remember: there's at least one in every family; if you can't figure out who it is, chances are it's you! So if you're in denial, this study is for you too!

This study is for anyone who wants to discover the roots of our biblical family tree, to trace the generations of Adam and Eve, Abraham and Sarah, Isaac and

Rebecca, Jacob and Esau, and Joseph and his brothers. It's for anyone who wants to ask the question, "Could God use my family to change the world?" As we read and study together, we'll learn that because the title "Child of God" belongs to us, this Genesis family is our family. And because of that, we are infinitely more blessed than broken.

Getting Started

For each week of our study there are five readings. Each of these readings includes the following segments:

Read God's Word A portion of the Bible story for the week, occasionally with other Scripture readings.

Reflect and Respond A guided reflection and study of the Scripture with space for recording your responses. (Boldface type indicates write-in-the book questions or activities.)

Pray About It A sample prayer to guide you into a personal time of prayer.

Act On It Ideas to help you act on what you have read. (Boldface type indicates write-in-the book questions or activities.)

You will be able to complete each reading in about 20-30 minutes. (You will need a pen or pencil and your Bible.) Completing these readings each week will help prepare you for the discussion and activities of the group session.

Once a week you will gather with your group to watch a video in which I share additional insights into the stories and their application for our lives. I encourage you to discuss what you're learning and to share how God is working in your own life and family. You will find that sharing with one another will enable you to recognize God's activity in your life even more clearly and help you encourage and pray for one another.

Before you begin this journey, give God permission to work on your heart and your life. Offer yourself to Him and express your desire for Him to bring restoration, healing, and blessing wherever it is needed in your life and the life of your family. May God richly bless you as you study His Word and discover how God can bring blessing from brokenness.

Blessings,

Jessica

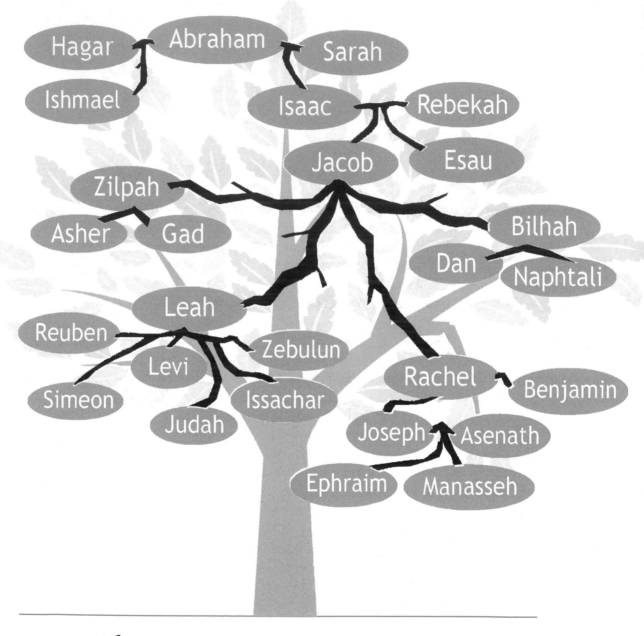

Abraham's Family Tree

Introductory Session
Video Viewer Guide

So God created humankind in his __image__ ,

in the image of God he created them;

__male__ *and* __female__ *he created them.*

Genesis 1:27 NRSV

When God wants to change the world, He starts with a __family__ .

When God wants to change the world, He starts with a family.

But when God wants to change a family, He starts with one __person__ .

The only way people will know how an __invisible__ God loves them

is if you love them first.

That is your most __important__ work.

Adam and Eve

My friend Tara knew from an early age that she was adopted. Even though she felt loved and accepted by her family, she always felt a sense of longing to know where she came from, to know her roots—her heritage. When people talked about their family histories, she would get a pang of longing to know her own history.

Once she was looking at some pictures of a friend and her mother, who at first glance didn't look that much alike. But when she looked closer, she saw that her friend's hands looked just like her mother's—a tiny piece of heredity hidden in the details. Tara wondered: Whose hands look like my hands? Whose laugh sounds like mine? All of this longing to know her origins was compounded by the fact that her adoptive father died when she was seven, and she had dreams about the man who had been her birth father. What did he look like? Did he ever think about her?

Finally, around the time she turned forty, Tara decided to stop wondering and do something about it. So she went to the courthouse in the county where she was born and asked for her original birth certificate, but the records were sealed. She learned, though, that somehow the system had overlooked one little clue. While the copy of the birth certificate she was issued did not have her birth parents' names, it did have a number. The same number possibly could be traced back through the records to locate her birth mother's name. She held her breath, wondering if this would lead to the meeting she had longed for.

In the basement of the courthouse, Tara discovered that the records from the 1960s were kept in huge, dusty books. She sat in a dimly lit room with the first yellowed book in front of her and followed her finger down the page—56 entries per page, 70,000 births in that state in 1965.

Since the records were arranged alphabetically by the mother's last name, a name she didn't have, she would have to manually examine each line in the records, scanning the six-digit numbers for one that matched her own. Her vision blurred after hours of gazing at books. She would sometimes come across a number that was just one digit off and would think for one second it was hers. Her heart jumped in her chest as if she had matched the numbers on a winning lottery ticket. But then she would realize it wasn't the right number and that she had to keep looking. She went back every day for five weeks.

Finally, one day when she was almost at the end of the alphabet, her finger landed on a number. She matched the digits one by one. She checked it again. Next to it she found her birth date and an F for female. Following the line back to the beginning she saw a last name—and then a first name: Suzanne. Tears welled up in her eyes as she said the name over and over again to herself.

When she went to make a copy of the page, her hands were shaking so much she couldn't work the copy machine. The clerk looked at her a little strangely as she helped her push the buttons. All she could say was, "I found my mother. My mother's name is Suzanne."

Each of us has an innate longing to know where we come from, to find out what makes us who we are. It's why children love to hear the story of the day they were born. It's the reason all those old family stories from long ago get told over and over again. Some of us can trace our lineage back only a few generations. Others know the events and names that began forming us centuries ago.

The truth is that if we all search far enough back, following generations up the family tree, each of us will eventually find the same family—the same story. Open your Bible to Genesis 1. This is your story, the story of where you came from. Trace your finger over that first sentence as if you, like Tara, were discovering the roots of your story for the very first time. "In the beginning."

Our study begins where the Bible begins, with creation. This is the beginning of the earth we all call home and the God who made it. Into this home that God constructs for His children, He places a family that will become your family and mine, the relatives that tie every single person you encounter in the world together. This is a story you should take personally.

This is where your story starts. This is where your family begins.

Day 1: God's Job Description

Read God's Word

¹ In the beginning God created the heavens and the earth. ² Now the earth was formless and empty, darkness was over the surface of the deep, and the Spirit of God was hovering over the waters.

Genesis 1:1-2

Reflect and Respond

Tara wasn't just searching for a number or a name. She was searching for a relationship. That discovery in the basement of a rural courthouse wasn't the end of her search; it was just the beginning.

Tara did some searching online and found a Suzanne with the last name from the record book who lived near the city where she had been born. After a few days and several drafts, she hand-wrote a letter on special paper, said a prayer, and stuck it in the mail.

In reply Tara received an email from a woman who was guarded at first. She asked, "What makes you think I'm the woman you're looking for?" Tara sent her a photocopy of the page from the courthouse book along with an essay she had written about being adopted and searching for her family.

The email she received in reply said, "You're a wonderful writer. Your father was, too." Tara's breath caught in her throat at those words: "Your father."

The emails began to warm up a bit, becoming more curious and friendly. She sent Tara a birthday card a few weeks later. As Tara put it later, "It was a huge deal to get that card."

Cards, emails, and an awkward but happy phone call shaped their gradually unfolding relationship. Suzanne was happy to fill in some blanks for Tara as they got to know one another, but she wasn't ready quite yet for face-to-face contact. This would be a huge deal for Suzanne too, one she hadn't believed would ever happen.

Suzanne did, however, pass along information about Tara's birth father. In response to another carefully composed letter, Tara quickly got another email in reply, this one from her birth father, the man whose face she had dreamed about since she was a child. The first two sentences made her heart skip a beat: "This is epic. I've been waiting forty years for this letter." He signed the first email, "Love, Frank." A few emails later he began signing them, "Love, Dad."

He sent her a picture of him from years earlier holding her half-sister in his lap when she was a little girl. After staring at that picture for a long time, Tara noticed his hand resting on the girl's shoulder. In an instant she realized, "His hand looked exactly like mine. I can't tell you what that was like. Finally there was a piece of me in someone else. Those are my hands."

Tara was trying to figure out how to save enough money for plane tickets for her, her husband, and the kids to fly to California to meet this family she never knew. When her dad learned she couldn't afford it, he purchased tickets for her whole family and sent them to her. When I last talked to Tara, she was giddy and nervous as she anticipated looking into her father's eyes for the first time.

Opening the Book of Genesis is like unsealing the records of our origins. It's being introduced to the family that marks our beginnings. This is who we are—our background, our family history. Our hearts long for this glimpse into the past, but not just to discover information or facts. Just as Tara wanted to know her birth mother and father—to have a relationship with them—we, too, want a relationship—to know the One behind it all, the Father we've been longing for.

The word *Genesis* literally means "beginning." If you open a Latin translation of the Bible, the first word is *Genesis*, which comes from the Greek, meaning "origin, creation."[1] Even the Hebrew word that begins the Bible, *bere'shit*, is a word that we have translated as the phrase "In the beginning."[2] That's what our hearts long to discover: our beginnings. But if we're honest, the specifics we find in Genesis may seem a bit vague for our taste.

My undergraduate degree is in biology, a discipline I chose because I have always felt close to God when admiring the intricate details of His creation. Genesis begins with the story of creation, but let's face it: it's short on details. When I read the creation story, the biologist in me wants to know *how*? How did all this happen? How does it fit with science: the fossil record, evolutionary theory, the existence of other planets? How long did it really take?

But when I search this story for the details of *how*, what I discover instead is that this story is all about the *who*. After the first word, *bere'shit* or *Genesis* ("In the beginning"), the very next word is *elohim*, God.[3] In the beginning, God. Instead of starting us out with *how, why*, or *what*, Genesis begins with *Who*—and that *Who* will be the central emphasis of our study together.

From its first verse, Genesis is a book of beginnings. It is deeply concerned with the origins of things—of the universe, humankind, relationships, sin, families, civilization, and one special family created and chosen by God to be the instrument through which He would bless the world. All of the things we see and experience in this world have their beginnings in Genesis—all except one: God. In a story of origins, we are introduced to a God who has no beginning and no end. When we open the first page, He's already there. Everything else has to be created from the ground up, with God as its beginning-less creator.

Read the following Scriptures and note what they tell us about God:

Psalm 93:2 God is everlasting

Isaiah 40:28 God is everlasting, Creator of all the earth, he never grows weak or weary, + no one can measure the depths of his understanding

Revelation 22:13 God is the Alpha + the Omega, the 1st + last, Beginning + End

In Genesis 1, there is no question of Who is in charge. God is the creator, and this is His creation. God stands in stark contrast to the material He's working with—His personality the opposite of the murky stuff He uses as raw material.

Reread Genesis 1:2 and fill in the blanks:

Now the earth was formless *and* empty*,* darkness *was over the surface of the deep.*

It's a good thing that God loves a challenge, because this place clearly isn't going to whip itself into shape. It's formless (chaotic), empty, and dark.

When you hear those three words, what images come to your mind? Think about what is formless (chaotic), what is empty, and what is dark.

It is in this chaotic, empty, dark place that God begins to create.

Write Genesis 1:3 below:

Then God said, "Let there be light" and there was light.

What a method! Instead of pulling the earth out of a hat, magician-style, God spoke things into being. I don't know about you, but that's a superpower I could use. *And she said: "Let the table be cleared and the dishes cleaned." And the kitchen was cleaned down to the last spotless glass!* The power to create with words is the first astounding act we see God complete. It's a power like no one else in the universe possesses. From the beginning we can see that this *Who* is an amazing being.

As Genesis 1:3 tells us, the first thing God spoke into being was light. It was an important starting point.

Read 1 John 1:5. What does this verse tell us about God?

God is light, & there is no darkness in him at all.

From the beginning we see that God and darkness are at odds with each other. God will not let darkness rule the earth. Where there is darkness in our lives, in our families, and in our world, we can be assured that God is speaking there, working to bring light in places of trouble and despair.

Lighting darkness is just the first step. If God's creating work is to make something from chaos, emptiness, and darkness, then we can use the opposites of these characteristics to piece together a job description of sorts for Him:

- God forms chaos into order;
- God fills emptiness;
- God lights darkness.

If we see the Bible as the story of God's actions in the universe, what we find is that from the very beginning God is forming, filling, and lighting. This is His job description throughout Scripture from the first day to the end of time.

This is the message we have heard from him and proclaim to you, that God is light and in him there is no darkness at all.
1 John 1:5 NRSV

Read the following Scriptures and note beside each how God forms (brings order from chaos), fills, or lights:

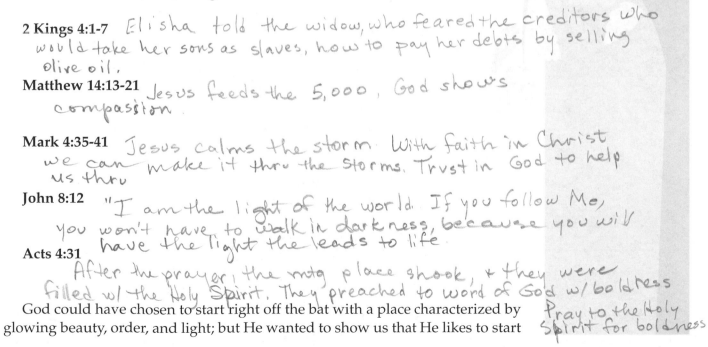

2 Kings 4:1-7 *Elisha told the widow, who feared the creditors who would take her sons as slaves, how to pay her debts by selling olive oil.*

Matthew 14:13-21 *Jesus feeds the 5,000, God shows compassion.*

Mark 4:35-41 *Jesus calms the storm. With faith in Christ we can make it thru the storms. Trust in God to help us thru.*

John 8:12 *"I am the light of the world. If you follow Me, you won't have to walk in darkness, because you will have the light the leads to life.*

Acts 4:31 *After the prayer, the mtg place shook, & they were filled w/ the Holy Spirit. They preached to word of God w/ boldness.*

Pray to the Holy Spirit for boldness.

God could have chosen to start right off the bat with a place characterized by glowing beauty, order, and light; but He wanted to show us that He likes to start

15

with raw material. That's good news for those of us who are still a diamond-in-the-rough. It's good news for imperfect families, for struggling relationships, for lives that can't quite seem to get it together, and for a world that is unraveling at the seams. When God wants to create the remarkable, He chooses to work with the less-than-perfect. As our Genesis family story unfolds, we will be grateful for that simple fact, since the family He chose and blessed was perfectly imperfect—and every family since has been as well.

As we'll soon find out, Genesis is the story of one family. If God wanted to start the world with a human experiment, He could have chosen to fill creation with people. Or He could have started slowly with just one person for the first lifetime or so to see how the experiment would work out. Instead He chose to start the world with a family. This tells us that God loves people and that God loves families.

We will soon learn that the first humans are given the command to "Be fruitful and multiply and fill the earth and subdue it" (Genesis 1:28 NRSV). This is actually God's first blessing of humankind—the command to fill the earth and to subdue it—a word that could mean to subdue the chaos they find there, to civilize its wildness, acting as God's agents on earth of forming order (subdue) and filling (be fruitful). Later we will find out that we have a vocation to light the world as well.

Look up Matthew 5:14 and write it here:

You are the light of the world - like a city on a hilltop that cannot be hidden.

In biblical terms we could say that if God's job description from Genesis 1:2 and throughout Scripture is to form and fill and light, then He deputizes the human family to be His agents on earth. God does some of His best work through the human family. Families exist to form and fill us and to light the darkness of the world with a radiant display of love and acceptance.

In the best of circumstances, families are the instruments through which God forms, fills, and lights our existence. In the worst circumstances, we find in them chaos, emptiness, and darkness. If we are honest, all of our families are the framework by which we live out the worst and best moments in our lives. There is nothing closer, nothing more personal, nothing that pushes our emotional buttons more—for good and bad—than our families.

How has your family formed you?

What did your family fill you with or instill in you?

Has there been a time when family (blood-related or chosen) has been a light in the dark world for you?

This chaotic, empty, dark place in which creation happens is rough material. Some of our families have rough material in them as well. Some of us have been formed in ways that were in reaction to hurtful words or actions. Some of us were filled with more negative messages about ourselves than blessings. While for many the family is a place of light and warmth, for others their picture of family is a place where darkness overshadows hope. The good news is that wherever there is chaos, wherever there is emptiness, wherever there is darkness, there is God.

Following this description of the raw material of the new world as formless, empty, and dark is the very last phrase that trumps it all: "and the Spirit of God was hovering over the waters" (Genesis 1:2). I love what a challenge this word *Spirit* is to translate. In Hebrew it's the word *ruakh*, a word that means Spirit but also can mean wind or breath.[4] Where there is chaos, there is God—hovering, waiting, forming a plan to make ordinary raw material into something extraordinary because of the presence of His Spirit there.

God's Spirit never leaves us, even in our most difficult times.

Read Psalm 139:7-12. What are some of the places and actions listed that cannot hide us from the presence of God?

heaven
to the grave   *farthest ocean*
ride the wings of the morning   *darkness*

What would you add to this list from your own life experience?

If God was present before all creation, there is no place that we can flee from or hide from Him. No situation is too chaotic, empty, or dark for Him. Where we find struggles, darkness, imperfection, and the rawest of raw material, we can be sure that God is there, ready to act—speaking light and love to create something beautiful.

Pray About It

God, I am so thankful that You love new beginnings. When I am overwhelmed by the chaos, emptiness, and darkness I see in this world, remind me that You are here, bringing order, fullness, and light. Help me to offer You the raw material of my life and my family so that You may use them to create something beautiful. Amen.

> The good news is that wherever there is chaos, wherever there is emptiness, wherever there is darkness, there is God.

Jay Sekulow

Act On It

- Do some research into your family of origin this week. Call or write an older relative and ask him or her to tell you a story about the family. Or look through some old pictures or letters and take a moment to remember those stories yourself. Consider where you see God at work in your family's past.

Day 2: Home-Maker

Read God's Word

1 ¹*In the beginning God created the heavens and the earth.* ² *Now the earth was formless and empty, darkness was over the surface of the deep, and the Spirit of God was hovering over the waters.*

³ *And God said, "Let there be light," and there was light.* ⁴ *God saw that the light was good, and he separated the light from the darkness.* ⁵ *God called the light "day," and the darkness he called "night." And there was evening, and there was morning—the first day.*

⁶ *And God said, "Let there be a vault between the waters to separate water from water."* ⁷ *So God made the vault and separated the water under the vault from the water above it. And it was so.* ⁸ *God called the vault "sky." And there was evening, and there was morning—the second day.*

⁹ *And God said, "Let the water under the sky be gathered to one place, and let dry ground appear." And it was so.* ¹⁰ *God called the dry ground "land," and the gathered waters he called "seas." And God saw that it was good.*

¹¹ *Then God said, "Let the land produce vegetation: seed-bearing plants and trees on the land that bear fruit with seed in it, according to their various kinds." And it was so.* ¹² *The land produced vegetation: plants bearing seed according to their kinds and trees bearing fruit with seed in it according to their kinds. And God saw that it was good.* ¹³ *And there was evening, and there was morning—the third day.*

¹⁴ *And God said, "Let there be lights in the vault of the sky to separate the day from the night, and let them serve as signs to mark sacred times, and days and years,* ¹⁵ *and let them be lights in the vault of the sky to give light on the earth." And it was so.* ¹⁶ *God made two great lights—the greater light to govern the day and the lesser light to govern the night. He also made the stars.* ¹⁷ *God set them in the vault of the sky to give light on the earth,* ¹⁸ *to govern the day and the night,*

and to separate light from darkness. And God saw that it was good. [19] And there was evening, and there was morning—the fourth day.

[20] And God said, "Let the water teem with living creatures, and let birds fly above the earth across the vault of the sky." [21] So God created the great creatures of the sea and every living thing with which the water teems and that moves about in it, according to their kinds, and every winged bird according to its kind. And God saw that it was good. [22] God blessed them and said, "Be fruitful and increase in number and fill the water in the seas, and let the birds increase on the earth." [23] And there was evening, and there was morning—the fifth day.

[24] And God said, "Let the land produce living creatures according to their kinds: the livestock, the creatures that move along the ground, and the wild animals, each according to its kind." And it was so. [25] God made the wild animals according to their kinds, the livestock according to their kinds, and all the creatures that move along the ground according to their kinds. And God saw that it was good.

[26] Then God said, "Let us make mankind in our image, in our likeness, so that they may rule over the fish in the sea and the birds in the sky, over the livestock and all the wild animals, and over all the creatures that move along the ground."

[27] So God created mankind in his own image,
    in the image of God he created them;
    male and female he created them.

[28] God blessed them and said to them, "Be fruitful and increase in number; fill the earth and subdue it. Rule over the fish in the sea and the birds in the sky and over every living creature that moves on the ground."…

[31] God saw all that he had made, and it was very good. And there was evening, and there was morning—the sixth day.

2 [1] Thus the heavens and the earth were completed in all their vast array.

[2] By the seventh day God had finished the work he had been doing; so on the seventh day he rested from all his work. [3] Then God blessed the seventh day and made it holy, because on it he rested from all the work of creating that he had done.

Genesis 1:1-28, 31; 2:1-3

Reflect and Respond

When Jim proposed marriage to me in the "Christian Living" aisle of a bookstore, the countdown began. It was nine months and eight days from our engagement to our wedding, a whirlwind of planning. Months of wedding arrangements meant lots of opinions from friends and relatives about what a wedding should be like. When I told my mother I was weary of all the wedding advice, she rolled her eyes and laughingly responded: "Just wait until you have children!"

Many wedding customs in our country have stayed the same over the years; others have changed dramatically. I'm intrigued by the marriage practices of first-century Jewish families. Their version of engagement was actually a binding contract, with the fathers of both the bride and groom agreeing to the union, the bride accepting a proposal, an exchange of a gift from groom to bride, and then the seal of a toast with a glass of wine. After that, the bride and groom were bound together just as a married couple is bound together in our day. They took betrothal so seriously that cancelling a wedding was the equivalent of divorce.

One of the major differences between their culture and ours is that our engagements are often spent preparing for the wedding—hard work that, let's face it, falls mostly on the bride. For the first-century Jewish couple, however, the hard work after the engagement was for the groom. With the betrothal in place, the only things standing between the couple and marriage were a ceremony and a house. Immediately after the engagement, the groom began planning and building a home for his future wife and family. When it was completed he could tell his bride that their home was ready and the wedding ceremony could begin.

First the home. Then the family. That's the order that Genesis takes as well. The first chapter of Genesis is dedicated to God building a home: our world. Only when the environment is complete do the human inhabitants move in.

God's job description of forming, filling, and lighting the world are clearly seen in this first chapter. He takes three days to order chaos, preparing environments, and then three days to fill emptiness, creating the inhabitants that belong there. Days 1–3 are a picture of the home; days 4–6 are a description of the family.

Fill in this table with a few words that describe God's creation on each day:

Environments Created		Inhabitants Created	
Day 1 Gen. 1:3-5	light – day dark – night	**Day 4** Gen. 1:14-19	sun moon stars
Day 2 Gen. 1:6-8	sky water	**Day 5** Gen. 1:20-23	birds creatures of the sea
Day 3 Gen. 1:9-13	land vegetation	**Day 6** Gen. 1:24-25 / Gen. 1:26-31	1. livestock & wild animals 2. man

It's clear that this pattern is no accident. The first three days of creating environments (ordering chaos) are meant to line up with the next three days of creating inhabitants (filling emptiness). The space created on Day 1 (the light and dark) is filled with the inhabitants of sun, moon, and stars. The environments created on Day 2 (the sky above and sea below) are filled with the inhabitants of fish and fowl. The environment created on Day 3 (dry land) is filled with the inhabitants of land animals and, finally, human beings.

Each of these created inhabitants would have a special relationship with the environment it was created to fill. And no being would have such a unique or more connected relationship with its environment as the human family.

The poetry of Genesis 1 means that there are patterns here that repeat again and again to draw our attention to the beauty and design of creation.

Take a look at today's Scripture (pages 18 and 19) and circle or underline the places you see the patterns listed below. If you're feeling creative, you can mark each phrase or pattern with a different symbol or color.

- **"And God said"**
- **"And there was evening and there was morning, the _____ day"**
- **God saw that it was good or very good.**
- **The act of separating or gathering into two separate things.**

This idea of creation by separation intrigues me. God orders the chaos by separating each aspect into its own realm. It reminds me of the way I try to order the chaos of our own family's environment—separating out toys into different bins in the playroom, separating the lights and darks before they go into the wash, separating the trash and recycling. The business of ordering chaos to make a home inhabitable is one that began this very first week of creation!

God's acts of separating chaos and making order take place when He contains darkness by separating it from light. He separates the waters above and below and creates an environment in the middle where there's some breathing room. Lastly, He separates the dry land from the water, creating an inhabitable space.

Each of the created animals is separated from the others, categorized in a way by being given its own day of creation. Human beings are clearly seen as special from the beginning, separated into their own category apart from the other life forms to indicate that we will have a special place in creation.

This home, this creation, is now filled with family. Environments have been ordered from chaos. Inhabitants have filled the emptiness. Light fills it all. God fills it all. From the very beginning, we see that He is present and active and interested. He is invested in His creation. And He is finished.

The last day of creation, Day 7, is not a day for ordering or filling.

Reread Genesis 2:2-3. What is this a day for?

Rest, holy

Here is another form of creation by separation. God separates the last day from the previous six. He makes it different by not working. He creates it by not creating. The text tells us that he makes the seventh day "holy." This is the first time we've heard this concept of holiness, but it won't be the last. The term simply means that this day is different, separated from the other days, consecrated for a special purpose. Later we'll learn that as people who love and have faith in this God, we are called to be holy as well. We will be separated out for a purpose, and that purpose will not only bring order and light to our lives but will spill over to bring order and light to creation itself.

The picture of God resting on the seventh day reminds us of God's value to our universe in the creation story. God is not important because of the work He does—the *what*. His importance is not in the miraculous way He does that work—the *how*. The value and idea at the center of this story is the *Who*, God Himself. On the seventh day He is present, and that presence is a gift just as everything He formed in the first six days is. In fact, God's presence is the greatest gift those of us who live in creation will receive.

> God's presence is the greatest gift those of us who live in creation will receive.

Read Exodus 20:8. What command are we given in this verse?

Remember to observe the Sabbath day by keeping it holy.

When we have a chance to participate in the Sabbath that God created, it's a reminder to us that our worth is not found in our work (what we do) or our skill (how we do it), but in who we are to God. We are valuable to God because He created us and loves us, not because of anything we do or don't do.

Describe how you can honor the Sabbath that God created on the seventh day:

What does it feel like when you spend time at rest with God?

peace
centered & refocused

The day the Jewish groom completed the house would have to be the day he had been looking forward to all along because it meant he finally got to be with his bride. As he began his journey back to her home to share the news and begin the wedding ceremony, the first tradition of the wedding celebration began. Friends who noticed where he was going would run ahead, shouting a single phrase over and over until they reached her house, and then shouting it outside her window: "The bridegroom is coming! The bridegroom is coming!"

First a home. Then a family. This creation, this home, was prepared for us, prepared with purpose and care by a Bridegroom who longed to live in it side by side with the bride He was creating for Himself.

Pray About It

Creator God, thank You for the way You've shaped our earthly home and for the way You promise to live in it with us. Grant me the grace to help care for it well. Help me to separate out time for rest with You, and use that time to make me holy. Amen.

Act On It

• Spend some time in God's creation today. Examine the big picture and the little details. Where do you see the grandness of God? Where do you see His care for the smallest specifics of creation? Spend some time thanking Him for His handiwork.

Day 3: The Divine Picture Frame

Read God's Word

¹⁹ Now the LORD God had formed out of the ground all the wild animals and all the birds in the sky. He brought them to the man to see what he would name them; and whatever the man called each living creature, that was its name. ²⁰ So the man gave names to all the livestock, the birds in the sky and all the wild animals.

But for Adam no suitable helper was found. ²¹ So the LORD God caused the man to fall into a deep sleep; and while he was sleeping, he took one of the man's ribs and then closed up the place with flesh. ²² Then the LORD God made a woman from the rib he had taken out of the man, and he brought her to the man.

²³ The man said,

"This is now bone of my bones
and flesh of my flesh;
she shall be called 'woman,'
for she was taken out of man."

[24] That is why a man leaves his father and mother and is united to his wife, and they become one flesh.

Genesis 2:19-24

Reflect and Respond

Imagine that you're touring the headquarters of a large, powerful corporation. You're excited to see behind the scenes where something of such global significance is created from the ground up. You visit the lobby, the bustling mailroom, the grand boardroom, and the various offices. As you notice the offices getting bigger and the décor more lavish, you find yourself standing outside the door of the office of the corporation's head, the CEO.

The suite takes up half of the top floor with its dark mahogany interior, displaying awards, gifts from dignitaries, and photos of the boss with famous people. On the grand desk there's a single picture frame. In this setting reflective of rank and position, you want to see what picture sits in the most honored place of all. When you finally crane your neck to get the best viewing angle, there it is: a picture of two children, a girl and a boy, the CEO's family. The contrast to the atmosphere of power is stark: these two smiling faces where an influential and powerful person can gaze at them all day.

The placement of that picture tells quite a bit about the person who sits at that desk. It says: "No matter how important the work we do here, no matter how much money passes through our hands or how much global impact we have, I know what is really important. This is what's important to me. They are the reason behind my life, and everything I do here is with them in mind."

Genesis 1 and 2 act as a kind of global tour for us. We get to see the world from its beginnings on a grand scale. The lavish work that God is capable of takes our breath away. But a close look at the details shows us what is closest to God's heart: His children. Leon R. Kass says, "Man is the ultimate work of creation: he is the last of the creatures listed in hierarchic order, and once he appears, the work of creation is complete."[5]

When we look at the scale of creation, it's astounding that God felt a need to make someone who would communicate with Him, someone who would be made in His image, who would be called His child to be cherished and loved. What do we see in the picture frame on God's desk of creation? What's His most prized creation? The human family. And what do we learn about our family?

1. We are made in God's image.
2. We are made with a connection to our home and to our Creator.
3. We are made for each other.

Let's look more closely into that frame—the one where God keeps us close to His heart—and find what each of these insights reveals about us.

1. We are made in God's image.

The story of the creation of human beings stretches between Chapters 1 and 2 of Genesis. Each chapter has its own distinct account of how the world came to be. They are different in many ways, but each highlights humanity as the pinnacle, the masterpiece of God's already remarkable work.

Our first view into the picture frame on God's desk comes in Genesis 1:27: "So God created humankind in his image, in the image of God he created them; male and female he created them" (NRSV). Human beings are made in God's image. The Hebrew word for *image* here is *tselem*, which means to cut off, or to chisel.[6] We are, in one sense, a chip off the old block of the God of the universe.

What do you think it means to be created in God's image?

Students of this passage have come up with many lists of what it may mean for us to be made in the image of God. Some have written about humanity's unique ability within the animal kingdom to love, to forgive, to have the power of speech and reason, to exercise judgment and decision making, and to have the freedom to imagine and create. Whatever belongs on this list, this portrayal of our origins is not something to be taken lightly. We are the only part of creation given this honor, the only creatures that carry the image of the Creator. When we notice that something is an image of something else (a photograph, sculpture, painting), we can see that it not only resembles it but also points to the model, reminding those who look at it that the original is something grander and more beautiful. Like the work of art that we are, the Creator intended that we should retain and resemble His image. And when we consider other human beings, no matter how likable or unlikable, we are to remember that they are made in His image as well.

As image-bearers of our Creator, what are the attributes of God that we can display? Read these verses and note some clues you find there.

Psalm 116:5 *Kindness, goodness, merciful*

Philippians 2:6-7 *humble*

Gracious is the Lord, and righteous; our God is merciful.
Psalm 116:5
NRSV

25

Colossians 3:13 *forgiveness*

1 John 4:8 *love*

2. We are made with a connection to our home and to our Creator.

In the creation story of Genesis 2, we are given much more detail about the story of the creation of the human family.

Read Genesis 2:7. From what is the first human created?

from the dust of the ground

> *Then the LORD God formed man from the dust of the ground, and breathed into his nostrils the breath of life; and the man became a living being.*
> Genesis 2:7 NRSV

The phrase "formed a man from the dust" is the English translation of the Hebrew verb *yatsar*, the same word we would use to describe a potter's actions as he forms shapeless clay into a beautiful vessel.[7] This is a supremely "forming" act, fitting perfectly into God's job description of forming, filling, and lighting the universe. God forms a human being from the ground itself, the most common material to be found.

The word for *ground* in Hebrew is *adamah*,[8] and the word for *human*—not the male word *man* but *human*, the word that encompasses both male and female—is *adam*.[9] That's where the first person gets his name, Adam, which means "human."

That kind of word play, from *adamah* to *adam*, lets us know that of all the environments to be filled with inhabitants, God is doing something special here to give humans a significant connection with their environment, the earth. We will soon see that when humans flourish, their environment benefits. When humans sin, their environment suffers along with them.

Dirt is not the only part of the recipe that makes a human.

According to the second part of Genesis 2:7, what does God do to complete His human creation?

breathed breath of life into his nostrils

Into this dusty creature, as common as the ground we walk on, God breathes the breath of life. Suddenly we are not simply ordinary. We are infused with God's own breath, the same breath that hovered over the waters in Genesis 1. We learn something very special about ourselves in this passage—about the balance of our ordinariness and the extraordinary God Who fills us with life. In an already incredible world, there is something special about us.

Humans aren't just the inhabitants, filling the environment of earth. We're also an environment created for the One Holy Inhabitant to occupy, filling us with His image, His breath.

What does 1 Corinthians 6:19-20 tell us about ourselves?

our body is a temple of the Holy Spirit you must honor God by your body

What does it suggest should be our response?

quit eating all the junk and take care of your body

Of all the holy places on earth that God would choose to make His temple to live, He chose to dwell inside His people—inside you and me.

3. We were made for each other.

It's interesting that in the picture frame on God's desk of creation, there is not just one image. There are two children there—a set that is not identical but complementary. As good as creation may be (and it is very good), there is one last thing that is not good about it.

Read Genesis 2:18. What did God say was not good, and what was His solution?

Not good for man to be alone - He will make a helper just right for you

With all the creatures surrounding him, the human is alone because there isn't another one like him. Even the presence of God Himself doesn't quite fit the need for this specific kind of companionship that the *adam* longs for.

Genesis 2 refers twice to the need for a "suitable helper" (vv. 18, 20). The Hebrew word for helper or helpmate, *ezer* (pronounced AY-zur, rhyming with laser), was never intended to imply subservience. In fact, besides this use in Genesis 2, all of the other uses of *ezer* in the Bible refer to God as our helper.[10]

What do you learn from the following Scriptures about God being our ezer?

Exodus 18:4 *God helped rescue Moses from the sword of Pharoah.* *rescuer*

Deuteronomy 33:7 *Moses cried out to God to help the tribe of Judah* *defends*

Psalm 33:20-22 *God is our help & our shield.* *protects*

The LORD God said, "It is not good that the man should be alone; I will make him a helper as his partner." Genesis 2:18 NRSV

27

Humans are created to help other humans, to be ezers to them. The first two relationships on earth were intended for worshiping God and helping another human being. When we are living in the harmony that was created in Genesis, selfish ambition will be trumped by a desire to support others in our human family.

I recently attended a beautiful outdoor wedding under a blue sky. The bride and groom were both giddy with the joy of the day. The pastor performing the ceremony had a dual role: He was also the father of the bride. In that special position, his words of counsel and guidance to the bride and groom during the ceremony took on a very personal tone. One piece of wisdom for the bride and groom reflected our passage in Genesis so well. To both of them he gave this charge: "Love is meeting another person's need when it is uniquely in your power to do so." We are all given the calling of this relationship of service to others.

What instructions do we find in Philippians 2:3-4?

Don't be selfish, don't try to impress others. Be humble, thinking of others as better than yourselves. Don't look out for your own interests, but take an interest in others, too

The second human isn't created from the dirt; this time God takes a piece of the man himself. God performs the first surgery by removing Adam's rib and fashioning from it a whole new being.

Reread Genesis 2:23. What does Adam exclaim when he lays eyes on this new creature?

At last!

The story of creation is complete only when this last step of companionship is in place. Humanity is now living in the companionship of family. It is the first building block of the seven billion people who reside on our planet today. Beginning in Genesis 2, every new human being will start life by emerging from the flesh of another, brought into the world to help other humans and reside in joyful community in the presence of our creator God.

In even the most powerful "office" in the world, there is a clue to the Boss's heart. In God's workspace, you are the person in that picture frame. Made in His image, you are the likeness He loves to gaze upon. You are the center of His creation, the one He takes most pride in, the one He would do anything to protect from harm and salvage from destruction. If that doesn't wow you, it should. Even with the magnificent Himalayas, the breathtaking Grand Canyon, the speed of the cheetah, and the grandeur of the humpback whale, you are still His favorite—the pinnacle of creation.

"None [of us] is the full image of God alone. Only in community of humankind is God reflected." [11]
—Walter Brueggeman

Pray About It

Lord, thank You for creating us for relationship and for community. Help me to fulfill my role as helper to my fellow human beings. Amen.

Act On It

• **Take your role as ezer, or helper, seriously by finding someone you can serve. Do it secretly, without telling the person what you're doing or why.**

Day 4: My Original Sin

Read God's Word

¹ *Now the serpent was more crafty than any of the wild animals the* LORD *God had made. He said to the woman, "Did God really say, 'You must not eat from any tree in the garden'?"*

² *The woman said to the serpent, "We may eat fruit from the trees in the garden,* ³ *but God did say, 'You must not eat fruit from the tree that is in the middle of the garden, and you must not touch it, or you will die.'"*

⁴ *"You will not certainly die," the serpent said to the woman.* ⁵ *"For God knows that when you eat from it your eyes will be opened, and you will be like God, knowing good and evil."*

⁶ *When the woman saw that the fruit of the tree was good for food and pleasing to the eye, and also desirable for gaining wisdom, she took some and ate it. She also gave some to her husband, who was with her, and he ate it.* ⁷ *Then the eyes of both of them were opened, and they realized they were naked; so they sewed fig leaves together and made coverings for themselves.*

⁸ *Then the man and his wife heard the sound of the* LORD *God as he was walking in the garden in the cool of the day, and they hid from the* LORD *God among the trees of the garden.* ⁹ *But the* LORD *God called to the man, "Where are you?"*

¹⁰ *He answered, "I heard you in the garden, and I was afraid because I was naked; so I hid."…*

* * *

²¹ *The* LORD *God made garments of skin for Adam and his wife and clothed them.*

Genesis 3:1-10, 21

29

Reflect and Respond

Standing in the checkout line, I clutched the tail of my mother's shirt and let out a bored sigh. Nothing in this long trip through the grocery store had interested me—until now. I noticed that someone had placed an entire rack of colorful, tempting items right at my eye level. That's when I spotted it. The tag showed a picture of a girl with a large ball strapped to her wrist as she banged it like a punching bag. Her face reflected pure glee. Below, the bright red balloon quivered with potential, begging to be blown up. I needed, no, I deserved that balloon. Just as I turned to my mom to make my carefully worded plea, she shook her head, reminded me we were in a rush, and wheeled the shopping cart out to the parking lot, calling over her shoulder for me to follow.

I honestly don't remember what happened next. Did I forget that it was in my hand? Did I develop some devious plot? Whatever the cause, the next thing I knew, I was sitting in the backseat of the car with the balloon in my lap. All at once it hit me: I had sinned. I quickly stuffed it into my pocket, shame coloring my face. All the way home I was certain that the police were right behind us, that they had been tipped off by the clerk at the checkout: "That's her, officer, the one in the Scooby Doo T-shirt! She's the culprit."

At the house I slipped into the guest bathroom and concealed my sin at the bottom of a basket of magazines and then glanced both ways as I shut the door behind me to be sure no one had seen. For months my heart raced every time someone entered that bathroom, certain I would be found out. The colorful object of desire had deflated into a stone of shame in my heart, never to be played with.

Though I'm grown, I have to admit that my impulses still lead me astray sometimes. Often I don't even realize what they are until I've already "grabbed them off the rack."

How does this happen? How does something that starts so small—an idea, an urge—snowball into an act that leaves us ashamed, concealing our actions and throwing a wrench into our relationships?

One of the best descriptions of the path that leads us to the bottom of this pit can be found in Genesis 3. This story is essential because it's the story of not only the first sin but also every sin. It describes the anatomy of Eve's temptation, but it's our story too—a story about how, even when we start with the best of intentions, a single thought can develop into an act that upsets our entire world.

The anatomy of temptation can be traced from one of its parts to the next, all linked in an association of harmfulness. The head is the starting point. It sees and hears the possibilities and longs to taste the forbidden fruit. It also rationalizes, justifies, and makes up excuses. Sin would never happen unless we did the mental soft-shoe around the warning bells that go off when we are tempted.

The taste buds mark the moment of sin itself. So brief. So delicious. And then it's over. And regret sets in.

The body is where the actual consequences grow. Once we've ingested, we begin to feel the effects of our decision. Lives throb with remorse. Bellies ache with regret. We're stuck embodying the outcome of our choices.

Finally: the limbs. Sin never stays put. It grows outward to places beyond our control. No sin is private. It always reaches out, affecting others. It sprouts legs and runs beyond our reach. It grows arms and hurts the people we love.

Reread today's Scripture and identify the anatomy of temptation. Label the parts of the passage on page 29 with the appropriate body parts:

Head (starting point of temptation)
Taste buds (moment of sin)
Body (consequences grow)
Limbs (our sin affects others)

Eve and Adam's encounter with the serpent traces our human condition from head to toe. Every sin since has followed in their footsteps. Every relationship has been marred by the same consequences of blame and shame. And it all began so innocently, with a simple question.

What question does the serpent ask in Genesis 3:1?

Did God really say, "You must not eat from any tree in the garden?"

Each temptation actually starts with a question about God. Did He really say that? Did He mean it? Does He matter? Every sin begins with the idea that God might not have our best interests at heart—that the rules He has given us might keep us from all the fun. The serpent's words are, of course, a misquote. Even God's words can be twisted. All temptation is a subtle attack on the character of God. How we formulate our answer always boils down to this: will we trust Him or will we decide to play God ourselves?

After twisting God's words, the serpent's next tactic is a lie contradicting God: "'You will not certainly die, . . . For God knows that when you eat from it your eyes will be opened, and you will be like God, knowing good and evil'" (Genesis 3:4-5). The insinuation is that God is holding something back from His children and cannot be trusted to have our best interests at heart.

Think of a time you were tempted to believe something untrue about God or about yourself. How did you shake that temptation?

> All temptation is a subtle attack on the character of God.

Sin often proceeds from deception, from believing untruths about God or ourselves. But the thing about deception is this: there is no power in a lie unless we believe it. The time you are spending studying God's Word is so important on many levels, but one of the most important is that it plants truth in your heart so that deception cannot tempt you to believe a lie that God does not love you or that you are not worthy of that love.

Read 1 Peter 5:8-11.

What do these verses say about the character of the one who loves to lie? (vv. 8-9)

He prowls around like a roaring lion, looking for someone to devour.

What do they say about the purpose of the One who loves truth? (vv. 10-11)

He will restore, support & strengthen you & will place you on a firm foundation.

When the first sin finally happens the description itself is so brief, its moment on the taste buds so fleeting, that it lasts only one verse. Eve chooses to play God, deciding to take matters of what's best for her and her family into her own hands and onto her own lips—and then onto her husband's. And the world is forever changed. The consequences of that one action dominate the rest of the chapter and the rest of their lives—and ours.

On the other side of this untested relationship is God. The world is so new that the first man and woman have no idea how God will answer sin, how He will treat children who disobey His commands. There's simply never been a sin to provoke His reaction. Here is the first test of God's character in the history of the world.

All we have seen so far is a God who interacts with perfect children in a perfect world. We may wonder: How will He react when things go wrong? And what will God do when this imperfect world is filled with imperfect humans? This is the question for all of us to consider, since we all live outside of Eden and we all sin—we all face the moment of coming before Him broken, asking for another chance.

Adam and Eve stand before Him, vulnerable, exposed, naked, and ashamed. Will He be wrathful? Angry? Cold? Rejecting?

Reread Genesis 3:21. How would you describe God's response to their sin?

He helped them.

The moment of suspense is answered by the unexpected. Instead of wrath they are shown kindness. Instead of rejection, grace. Out of compassion God cares for them by clothing their nakedness, taking the scratchy, disposable fig leaves they've patched together and providing instead the first clothing the world has ever known—a wardrobe of grace.

What truth about God reassures you when you've messed up?

The anatomy of a temptation doesn't end in a body of shame. Head, taste buds, body, limbs—all is covered by the grace of God. This happened the very first time humans messed up, and it has been happening ever since.

I think of the way I wrap a towel around my son's shivering, damp body at the end of a bath. No matter what a stinker he's been that day, that's all on its way down the drain as I lift that little dripping body wrapped in a bundle into my lap to hold him close. He's almost the age I was when I committed my first (memorable) sin in the checkout line. But I want him to know early: *You have a choice every day, a choice of which voice to listen to, a choice to be good. And when you're not, I'll be here loving you just the same.*

God loves you and me just the same, too. No matter what kind of day we've had, no matter what kinds of choices we've made, His love and grace wash over us. I'm so glad He has proved His love again and again, from the very beginning.

Pray About It

Lord God, Your ability to love me just the same when I make good choices and when I make bad ones is humbling and beautiful. I am so grateful! Help me to reflect onto others the grace You give to me, so that they will know such a depth of love exists in Your world. Amen.

Act On It

- Is there a wrong you've committed that still brings pangs of guilt when it comes to your mind? Make a tangible prayer of confession today by writing down a word or drawing a symbol on a piece of paper that reminds you of that sin. Pray a private prayer, and then do something to destroy that paper in the same way God destroys your guilt.

No matter what kind of day we've had, no matter what kinds of choices we've made, [God's] love and grace wash over us.

Day 5: Cracks in the Windshield

Read God's Word

8 *Then the man and his wife heard the sound of the* Lord *God as he was walking in the garden in the cool of the day, and they hid from the* Lord *God among the trees of the garden.* 9 *But the* Lord *God called to the man, "Where are you?"*

10 *He answered, "I heard you in the garden, and I was afraid because I was naked; so I hid."*

11 *And he said, "Who told you that you were naked? Have you eaten from the tree that I commanded you not to eat from?"*

12 *The man said, "The woman you put here with me—she gave me some fruit from the tree, and I ate it."*

13 *Then the* Lord *God said to the woman, "What is this you have done?"*
The woman said, "The serpent deceived me, and I ate."

14 *So the* Lord *God said to the serpent, "Because you have done this,*

"Cursed are you above all livestock
  and all wild animals!
You will crawl on your belly
  and you will eat dust
  all the days of your life.
15*And I will put enmity*
  between you and the woman,
  and between your offspring and hers;
he will crush your head,
  and you will strike his heel."

16 *To the woman he said,*

"I will make your pains in childbearing very severe;
  with painful labor you will give birth to children.
Your desire will be for your husband,
  and he will rule over you."

17 *To Adam he said, "Because you listened to your wife and ate fruit from the tree about which I commanded you, 'You must not eat from it,'*

"Cursed is the ground because of you;

> *through painful toil you will eat food from it*
> *all the days of your life.*
> ¹⁸ *It will produce thorns and thistles for you,*
> *and you will eat the plants of the field.*
> ¹⁹ *By the sweat of your brow*
> *you will eat your food*
> *until you return to the ground,*
> *since from it you were taken;*
> *for dust you are*
> *and to dust you will return."*

²⁰ *Adam named his wife Eve, because she would become the mother of all the living.*

Genesis 3:8-20

Reflect and Respond

I was running late to my first job interview. I was following the gravel truck in front of me too closely, hoping the driver would get the message, when suddenly I heard a loud CRACK! A rock had bounced off my windshield and left a circular ding right in the middle, a tiny crack peeking out from its side. I thought hopefully, *I can still drive with that little imperfection there. Maybe it won't spread.*

Over the next few weeks, the tiny crack did spread, growing tributaries, which in turn grew their own. The blinding glare forced me to replace the windshield.

A single piece of fruit. A tiny crack in paradise. No one could have predicted the range of consequences of that first sin. Once again their story is our story as well—the mistake, the aftermath, the wishful thinking we all engage in when considering the outcome: *Maybe it's not that bad; maybe it won't spread.*

At the heart of a perfect garden there existed a collection of perfect relationships. Man and woman lived in loving harmony. Humans tended their environment while it supported them. And God walked with them in the garden.

When the woman tasted the forbidden fruit and offered it to her husband, who did the same, it didn't take long for those relationships to sting with the consequences of their actions. Ashamed, they hid from God, who called out for them.

Reread Genesis 3:11-13 and answer the following questions:

When God asked about their newfound guilt, whom did they blame?

the serpent

35

Does God know why they're hiding and ashamed? (v. 11)

yes

After blaming each other and God, do they confess their actions? (vv. 12-13)

yes

Adam pointed the finger at his wife and then right at God: "The woman *you* put here with me." Eve responded with a classic: "The devil made me do it." Though they played the blame game, each of them admitted to eating the fruit. What follows in Genesis 3 is a list of the effects of sin that we are still dealing with today.

Review Genesis 3:14-19 and describe the consequences for each:

serpent - crawl, eat dirt
woman - painful childbirth, desire husband who will rule over
man - cursed the ground, eat food from ground

Let's talk about each of these consequences in the opposite order in which they are announced. God's first commentary on how the cracks of sin will spread into human lives has to do with the perfect relationship humans have had with their environment, created to provide them with food and shelter and beauty.

God has placed the *adam* on the earth to enjoy and oversee God's good creation with only one restriction. With the breaking of that one rule comes the breaking of the simple and symbiotic relationship humankind has enjoyed with the earth. Here is the negative side of the close connection between *adam* (human) and *adamah* (ground). When one is broken, the other suffers.

Originally it was an environment so ecologically ideal that no one had to plant or water or weed. No one had to kill in order to eat. It was the best of all harmonized worlds. Now there will be struggle to produce. Now identity will be bound up in the question "So what do you do?" and humans will confuse their worth with productivity, earning, rank, and success. The prediction that the eating of the fruit will result in death becomes clearer here as well.

Reread Genesis 3:19. What does God say about how their lifecycle will end and where they will return?

return to the ground

We've seen that human relationships with God and their earthly home will be different in this post-sin world. God also explains how their relationship with each other will be affected. The woman is told that she will suffer consequences in an act that she has not yet even experienced: bearing children. God says, "I will make your pains in childbearing very severe; with painful labor you will give birth to children" (Genesis 3:16a). If this doesn't make you a little upset with Eve, it should! We have Eve to thank for labor pains, swelling, and bloating; for baby weight and postpartum depression. None of this was part of God's original plan. (Yet because we probably would have done the same thing in her situation, perhaps we should offer Eve some grace. God certainly did.)

If we naively believe that the pain of childbearing is limited to labor and delivery, then we'll be surprised by our panic in a child's first trip to the emergency room and by the ache of watching them get on the school bus for the first time. Along with the joy of watching our children grow will come late nights of waiting for them to come home followed by sleepless nights wondering if they'll ever leave the nest. Every parent knows the heartbreak of watching a child's heart break. Every parent would gladly take on a child's pain. "This is going to hurt me more than it hurts you" should be the first page in every parenting book.

Read Genesis 4:8 in the margin. How will Adam and Eve experience the ultimate pain of parenthood? *loss of a son*

Children are born through life with ongoing pushing, teaching, listening, loving, and grace. That's the lifelong, painful nature of childbearing. Parents suffer through it because the result—the chance to love a human being who, like themselves, is made in God's image—is so completely and undeniably worth it.

The other relationship that begins to show the cracks of consequences from sin is the one the woman shares with her companion, Adam. This has been the first model of human relationship, the gift of perfect human partnership created by God. Woman and man enjoy each other as perfectly matched companions. Now there exists a new gulf between them.

Reread Genesis 3:16b and fill in the blanks:

"Your *desire* will be for your *husband*, and he will *rule* over you."

The kind of desire described here is not a loving desire or even a sexual desire. This is the desire to control, to subdue, to dominate. Followed by the other half of the sentence, "he will rule over you," it means that both partners will struggle to exploit their relationship for their own gain, to control the other instead of enjoying the intimate bond and life of mutuality they began in God's perfect creation.

This same word used for *desire* is mirrored in the very next chapter of Genesis. Who is doing the "desiring" in Genesis 4:7? In this context, is *desire* a positive or negative word?

sin   negative

> Cain said to his brother Abel, "Let us go out to the field." And when they were in the field, Cain rose up against his brother Abel, and killed him.
> Genesis 4:8 NRSV

God's first blessing to His children, "Be fruitful and multiply. Fill the earth and subdue it," is now forever tainted with the pollution of human corruption.

Both the multiplying of relationships and the subduing of the earth just got a lot more difficult. Men and women will labor. Their relationships with God, their environment, and each other will all have difficulties, brokenness. Life is going to involve hard work from here on out.

Eve receives her name just after these pronouncements.

Reread Genesis 3:20. What does Eve's name mean? Do you think it's a gift or a curse in light of this story?

Mother of all living

Strangely enough, there is a glimmer of good news in this list of consequences, which is embedded in God's message for the serpent. The one who matched wits with human beings is now doomed to the life of a belly-crawling, dust-eating snake. The serpent will exist forever in enmity with the offspring of the woman. The strange message encoded here comes in the form of a pronoun.

Reread Genesis 3:15 and fill in the blanks: *serpent*

"And I will put enmity between you *we* *and the woman, and between your* *serpent* *offspring and hers;* ___He___ *will crush your head, and you will strike* ___his___ *heel."* *Eve's offspring*

You and *your* refer to the serpent, and *hers* refers to Eve. But what about "he" and "his"? The grammar police would pull us over for having a pronoun without an antecedent. This "he," God says, will be one of Eve's offspring. He will receive an injury from the serpent, but in turn, He will strike the decisive blow in the battle. And He will eventually crush the serpent once and for all.

What do we learn about Christ in Colossians 1:15-17?
Christ is the visible image of the invisible God. Supreme over all creation. Everything is created through him & for him. He holds all creation

What do these Scriptures say about the victory that is ours because of Christ? *together*

1 Corinthians 15:57
He gives us victory over sin & death through our Lord Jesus Christ.

Romans 8:2
Because you belong to Him, the power of the life-giving Spirit has freed you from the power of sin that leads to death.

Hebrews 7:25-27
Holy & blameless, unstained by sin He offered himself as the sacrifice for the people's sins.

> *For the law of the Spirit of life in Christ Jesus has set you free from the law of sin and of death.*
> Romans 8:2 NRSV

Inserted into the litany of consequences from the first sin we find a consequence the serpent probably didn't expect: that God will fight for His children. He will never give up on them, no matter how long and wide the cracks of their mistakes grow. God's grace spreads farther than the reach of any sin, filling in the cracks with mercy and forgiveness. There is no place outside the reach of God's love.

According to Romans 8:38-39, what can separate us from God's love?

nothing

So far we've learned a lot from the first family on earth. They've had flawless beginnings, a tempting proposal, and a big fall. Rather than feeling disappointed that God would begin the Bible with the story of an imperfect family, it gives me hope. If God continued to walk with them in a new and imperfect world, maybe there is hope for our families, too—the hope that only Christ can bring.

"All love causes pain," says Mary Pipher in her book on families, *The Shelter of Each Other*.[12] But with all the love and all the pain humans are bound to feel in this post-Eden world, I'm thankful that God, too, knows the pain of bearing imperfect children through life. I'm thankful, too, that He found a way from the beginning to plant His plan for rescue, His seed of grace, right at the moment of our first sin, right there in the garden so we could watch it grow.

Pray About It

Jesus, I am Your dearly loved, flawed child. Just like Adam and Eve, I need Your love and Your grace to live in an imperfect world. When I am afraid or anxious, remind me again that nothing will ever be stronger than the bond of Your love for me. Amen.

Act On It

- Today, say to at least two people: "Tell me about your family." Listen well. Then, if given a chance, tell them something about yours. Remember that transparency and openness with our own stories helps others feel they are not alone. Make sure to pray for those two people and their families before you sleep tonight.

> God's grace spreads farther than the reach of any sin, filling in the cracks with mercy and forgiveness.

Week 1
Video Viewer Guide

In the beginning God created. (Genesis 1:1-2)

In the beginning, the earth was:

formless   –   chaotic, without shape

empty   –   void, uninhabited

dark   –   without light

God creates _order_ out of chaos.

God _filled_ the emptiness.

God brings _light_ to banish the darkness.

Three important relationships God created that were broken:

Humans' relationship with their _environment_

Humans' relationship with _each_   _other_

Humans' relationship with _God_

They _hid_ from the LORD God among the trees of the garden. But the LORD God

called to the man, "Where are you?"

Genesis 3:8-9 NIV

In the beginning was the Word. (John 1:1-3)

Wherever there's darkness or chaos and emptiness, that's where Jesus can be found, too...

lighting the darkness

ordering the chaos

filling the emptiness

Week 2
Abraham and Sarah

David grew up in a time when long-held conventions of prejudice and racism were starting to change. His mother made a point to speak often to her sons about how it was wrong to treat anyone differently just because he or she looked different on the outside. She wanted them to know that all people, no matter if they look alike or different, are made in the image of God. On one occasion in particular they had a chance to see whether she would stand up for what she had taught them.

Their family had made the five-hour trip to visit David's grandmother for a family gathering. When they arrived, David's uncles (his father's two brothers) were there. As they were visiting, one of his uncles used the "N word" in conversation. David's mother asked him not to use such a demeaning word around her or her boys. The uncle hadn't thought much about his choice of words since, unfortunately, it was just a part of his everyday speech. But once he realized how much it was upsetting his sister-in-law, he decided to get a rise out of her. He made a game of dropping the offensive word into conversation and then glancing at her with mock remorse and saying, "I'm so sorry to offend you."

This went on for a while and then David's mother took his father aside in a back bedroom and said, "Bill, get the bags; put them in the car. We're leaving."

David's dad tried to placate her by explaining that his brother didn't mean anything by it, that he was just acting out of ignorance, and that she should ignore him. She agreed with him on one point: that his brother was ignorant. "But," she said, "I don't want my boys to be around that kind of ignorance."

So instead of staying for the weekend, they took their unpacked bags, loaded them in the car, along with their two sons, and began the five-hour trip home. They had only been there two hours.

That family story made a huge impact on David as he grew up. He learned not only from his mother's words but also from her actions that it is important to stand up for others who are being insulted or mistreated, even if they aren't there, even if they will never know you have defended their worth. He learned it is important to do the right thing even if it means taking a stand against your family.

This week we'll meet two people who represent a generation that walked away from their families to follow God. Abraham and Sarah were the first generation in their family to walk away from the polytheistic, idol-worshiping culture in which they were raised. They also had some very countercultural ideas about how the One True God they worshiped was calling them to spread blessing to the nations around them in a time when keeping resources within the family or clan was the norm.

But before we can get to Abraham and Sarah, we'll begin the week with their ancestor Noah, who raised his family in a way that went against the grain of the entire society around him.

God often calls our families to be different from those around us. He even may be calling you to be different in some way from the generations before you in your own family. Let Abraham and Sarah and their family introduce you to a story of blessing that began, for them, by breaking with the past.

Day 1: A Real Page-Turner

Read God's Word

*⁵ The L*ORD* saw how great the wickedness of the human race had become on the earth, and that every inclination of the thoughts of the human heart was only evil all the time. ⁶ The L*ORD* regretted that he had made human beings on the earth, and his heart was deeply troubled. ⁷ So the L*ORD* said, "I will wipe from the face of the earth the human race I have created—and with them the animals, the birds and the creatures that move along the ground—for I regret that I have made them." ⁸ But Noah found favor in the eyes of the L*ORD.*

⁹ This is the account of Noah and his family. Noah was a righteous man, blameless among the people of his time, and he walked faithfully with God. ¹⁰ Noah had three sons: Shem, Ham and Japheth.

¹¹ Now the earth was corrupt in God's sight and was full of violence. ¹² God saw how corrupt the earth had become, for all the people on earth had corrupted their ways. ¹³ So God said to Noah, "I am going to put an end to all people, for the earth is filled with violence because of them. I am surely going to destroy both them and the earth. ¹⁴ So make yourself an ark of cypress wood....

¹⁷ I am going to bring floodwaters on the earth to destroy all life under the heavens, every creature that has the breath of life in it. Everything on earth will perish. ¹⁸ But I will establish my covenant with you, and you will enter the ark— you and your sons and your wife and your sons' wives with you. ¹⁹ You are to bring into the ark two of all living creatures, male and female, to keep them alive with you. ²⁰ Two of every kind of bird, of every kind of animal and of every kind of creature that moves along the ground will come to you to be kept alive. ²¹ You are to take every kind of food that is to be eaten and store it away as food for you and for them."

²² Noah did everything just as God commanded him.

Genesis 6:5-14, 17-22

Reflect and Respond

I remember the children's Bible that was in the waiting room of my dentist's office when I was a child. Flipping through it made for a great distraction from the dreaded exam that awaited me. I always turned immediately to the beginning of that picture Bible, to the image of Adam and Eve in the garden. It seemed a little scandalous to me that they were naked in that picture, even though they were purposefully posed behind carefully placed foliage. In the picture Eve was holding an apple. Most artists have painted it as an apple, even though the Bible only describes it as a "fruit." I'm not sure I would have given up paradise for an apple. In my imagination, it must have been something chocolate covered!

The world's introduction to sin was represented by something so small, so seemingly insignificant. It was just one tiny piece of fruit. But here, at the beginning of human history, is what the Bible teaches about sin: A little bit can go a long way. By the next generation, the next sin that we read about is murder, a brother taking the life of his brother. That seems to be quite a leap!

For some reason the editors of the *Children's Picture Bible* decided to leave Cain and Abel out of the story, even though I'm sure a story of jealousy and murderous anger between siblings is something most kids could understand quite well. We'll explore the Bible's recurring theme of sibling conflict in Week 4.

Cain and Abel are only the second generation on earth, and already we have a story that ends in murder. Their story is only a small sample of what happens when humanity kicks God out of the driver's seat. In just ten generations, the cracks of sin will spread so widely that the entire human race is falling apart.

What does Genesis 6:5-6 tell us? *Everything was evil. God was sorry he made humans. It broke his heart. He would destroy every living thing.*

Did you notice all the adjectives emphasizing just how bad the situation has become? *Great* wickedness, *every* inclination of the heart, *only* evil *all* the time. This means that the virus of sin has spread its infection to every family and every individual. The state of humanity has deteriorated to such a low point that God regrets creating them in the first place. The purposes for which He made humankind are being trampled by people whose only goal is to please themselves. No one is focused on being a helpmate (*ezer*) to serve their fellow humans, worshiping their Creator, or taking joy in the *adamah*, the earth on which they live. They are living only for themselves, and things are falling apart.

The one bright spot in our unfolding story, the sole virtuous person in all of humanity, is a man named Noah.

Write the words used to describe Noah in Genesis 6:9: *righteous Only blameless person living on earth at the time walked in close fellowship w/ God*

Noah is a righteous man, blameless among the people of his time, and he walks faithfully with God. This description of spotless obedience stands out in stark contrast to the corruption of the world around him.

Write the words used in Genesis 6:5, 11-13 to describe everyone else on earth:

totally evil corrupt, filled w/ violence

The image of God placed within human character is still detectable in Noah and his offspring. So God's plan emerges: He will start humanity over with the only faithful family left on earth. He will "reboot" creation in an attempt to get back to the way things were in Eden.

Noah's story is the stuff Sunday school lessons and children's sermons are made of. I remember looking at the picture of the ark in the children's Bible at my dentist's office too, counting the animals two-by-two as they entered the ark. It didn't picture the crowds of people being covered by the water, their hands frantically reaching upward as the flood overtook them. This story is not as "G-rated" as we've presented it to be through the years.

We can only imagine God's heart breaking as He makes the tough decision to start over. This story reveals for the first time that God has emotions. God can regret. It also reveals that God is willing to spare humanity for the glimmer of goodness found in one family. God can hope. At the center of the universe is the heart of a God who is deeply affected by human choices. Our choices not only have the power to break commands and laws; they have the power to break the heart of God or to bring hope and pleasure to our Creator.

The thing that has always intrigued me about the story of the flood is the unusual description of the waters that overtake the earth.

Read Genesis 7:11-12. From where do the waters come?

_____ **Above**   ⌣ **Below**   ? **Both above and below**

Review Genesis 1:6-7. What similarity do you find here?

He made a space to separate waters of earth + heavens, called space sky

On the second day of creation, God separated the water above from the water below. This was one of His acts of forming order out of the chaos, preparing an environment on earth that He would soon lovingly fill with inhabitants. The description of the way the floodwaters overwhelm creation is an intentional reversal of the separation of waters on Day 2 of the creation story, with waters closing in from above and below. The effect those waters have on the earth shows them moving in an opposite direction of the separation of seas and dry land on Day 3. The closely bound relationship between the *adam* (human) and the *adamah* (earth) means that as sin takes over the human world, the natural world descends into the chaos from which it came. Chaos is taking over.

In what ways have you seen humanity's sin bring chaos on earth? Give an example from the news as well as a personal observation or experience.

> At the center of the universe is the heart of a God who is deeply affected by human choices. Our choices . . . have the power to break the heart of God or to bring hope and pleasure to our Creator.

When we try to rule the world on our own, chaos breaks out again. Emptiness reigns. Darkness falls. The good news is that while we live in a volatile and erratic world, God is predictable. Wherever there is chaos, we can always expect to find God at work creating order, stability, and wholeness.

After the flood, God works quickly to reestablish light, order, and fullness to the earth. Noah and his family emerge from the ark to receive a familiar-sounding blessing from God.

Read Genesis 9:7 and write the blessing below:

Now be fruitful & multiply, and repopulate the earth.

God sees the new beginning as a fresh start and makes a promise: He will never again destroy the earth through a flood. He hangs a beautiful rainbow in the sky between heaven and earth as a reminder of this covenant with His people.

Problem solved. Bad people: wiped out. Good people: saved. Earth: perfect again. Right?

Not for long. When we turn the page on a new scene, we find our hero, Noah, drunk, naked, and passed out in his tent. During the episode, Noah's son Ham dishonors his father and his family by taking a gander at his drunken dad and telling his brothers about it. Thus ends the myth of the perfect family.

By the time we get to Chapter 11, we see that the seed of sin in Noah's family has taken root, grown, and ensnared a fledgling civilization. By this time humans are no longer primitives wandering naked in a garden; they have begun to develop a society complete with one of the first pieces of technology: the brick. How they choose to use their new invention will reflect the bent of their human hearts.

Read Genesis 11:4. What do they decide to build and why?

a great city with a tower that reaches into the sky. This will make us famous and keep us from being scattered all over the world

Their use of new technology reveals that the greatest desire of their hearts is to glorify themselves, to lift up their own name, to stretch out their creation to the heavens in an effort to out-god God Himself. The outcome is exactly what they are hoping to prevent: they are scattered across the earth. But now, instead of the waters above and below crashing in on them, it is the communication barrier that comes crashing down on them for the first time. They are unable to understand one another. They babble.

Because Babel exposes a new level of impoverishment in human relationships, and because it happens to be found in Chapter 11 of Genesis, I sometimes think of it as the "Bankruptcy Chapter" of the Bible. There is nothing more bankrupt than grasping for something to give your life meaning and provision in a place

Extra Insight
Encounters with alcohol and other addictive substances have damaged families throughout time. Even families that seem perfect to an outsider are not exempt from a secret shame that they keep from public view. If your family is wrestling with a loved one's addiction, there is no shame in getting help by talking with your pastor, a counselor, or a trusted friend about steps that can lead to recovery and wholeness.

where none can be found. As long as we look to ourselves and our own resources for what only God can provide, we will always come up short.

The pattern that Genesis reveals is that where sin is concerned, what starts small spreads out and takes over. From fruit to ark, from Noah's binge to Babel, Genesis is up front with us, providing a clear picture of what happens to humanity when we are left to our own devices. From Genesis 3 to 11, humanity brushes off God's guidance and walks its own path.

The first part of the Bible establishes the great problem of humanity before it answers with God's solution. We have to understand how truly broken we are before we can understand just how remarkable God's response of blessing is.

It's the eleventh chapter, the eleventh hour. What will God do with a broken, bankrupt, Chapter 11 world? It's time to discover what God has in mind to restore the children He loves so dearly and the world they have damaged.

As we turn the page between Chapters 11 and 12 of Genesis, we see one of the biggest shifts in the entire Bible. Possibly the only page turn with more power is the one between the Old and New Testaments. The transition between these two chapters moves us from problem to solution, from a focus on all of civilization to one nuclear family, from the origins of the world to the stories of the next generations. So stay with me. We're about to turn the page that will turn all of history.

> We have to understand how truly broken we are before we can understand just how remarkable God's response of blessing is.

Pray About It

Lord, sometimes the world's problems overwhelm me. I'm thankful that You are not overwhelmed. Thank You for being the One to provide blessing greater than all the brokenness. Thank You for never giving up on us—for never giving up on me. Amen.

Act On It

- Think about the tough choice God faced when deciding whether or not to start all over again. Reflect on the idea that God has emotions—that He can regret, grieve, and hope.

- **How does today's lesson show that God is deeply affected by our choices?**

- **How does it feel to know that your choices have the power to grieve the heart of God or to bring hope and pleasure to your Creator?**

Day 2: Blessed to Be a Blessing

Read God's Word

¹ The LORD had said to Abram, "Go from your country, your people and your father's household to the land I will show you.

² "I will make you into a great nation,
    and I will bless you;
I will make your name great,
    and you will be a blessing.
³ I will bless those who bless you,
    and whoever curses you I will curse;
and all peoples on earth
    will be blessed through you."

⁴ So Abram went, as the LORD had told him; and Lot went with him. Abram was seventy-five years old when he set out from Harran. ⁵ He took his wife Sarai, his nephew Lot, all the possessions they had accumulated and the people they had acquired in Harran, and they set out for the land of Canaan, and they arrived there.

Genesis 12:1-5

Reflect and Respond

Yesterday we left our human family in Chapter 11—in a state of moral and relational bankruptcy—wondering how God would repair the cracks of sin that had spread throughout the growing civilization. Today we finally turn the page from problem to solution, but this is no small spill that can be wiped away with ease. A big mess calls for a big cleanup.

As we open Chapter 12, we find ourselves immediately scanning the horizon for the momentous counterattack God is mounting to reclaim His children from the chaos that keeps taking over. In order for God to fix the twisted shape of the world, He will need to come up with a secret weapon so big and so powerful that it can repair the damage that has been done and somehow stop this recurring cycle of degeneration that repeatedly leaves the world in such a mess. What will this secret weapon be? What will God use to change the world?

Reread Genesis 12, verses 1 and 4. To whom is God speaking here, and who is included in God's call?

Abram and Lot *(nephew)* *+ wife Sarai* *livestock* *all the people they had taken into his household at Haran*

At first glance, the answer we find in these verses may seem a little underwhelming. God's secret weapon is a family—one man and one woman with their future in God's hands. But if we look deeper, we'll see that this is God's specialty—using the weak to overcome the strong.

Throughout history God has begun great things with just one small family. The world begins with Adam and Eve. The exodus from Egypt begins with Moses, Aaron, and Miriam. The arrival of the incarnate Son of God on earth opens with Mary and Joseph. When God wants to change the world, He starts with a family. Abraham and Sarah. (They're called Abram and Sarai here, but God changes their names later. You can explore why God changed their names in my Bible study *Namesake*.)

Do Abraham and Sarah realize that the future of the human race rests on their shoulders? Probably not. But in their first divine conversation, God offers them an opportunity to reshape human history.

Reread Genesis 12:1-3 in today's Scripture (page 49). What are God's instructions and promises to Abram? Underline the things that God promises He will do. Circle the things God commands Abram to do.

What do you observe?

blessings *How did he speak to him?*

Similar to His exchanges with Adam and Noah, God initiates conversation with words of both challenge and blessing. Despite the continuing state of the brokenness of the world and humankind, isn't it a relief to know that God's posture toward His children is still one of continual blessing? God longs to bless His children. His desire to bless was instrumental in the creation of the world. Now it will have much to do with the healing of the world as well.

Review Genesis 1:28, 9:1-3, and 12:1-3. What are the blessings we've seen God offer humans so far?

bearing children, fish, birds, animals, food, green veggies, Abram's blessings

What similarities or differences do you see in these three blessings?

Everything will be blessed through you

Here is God's chosen method to change the world: He will bless this family so that through them blessings will flow out to the rest of the world. This family will be God's instrument of blessing, His conduit of grace.

There's a big difference between a conduit and a container. A few years ago I had an amazing opportunity to visit the Holy Land, traveling around Israel and Palestine to visit sites of biblical events. One of the most impactful days was our visit to the Jordan River. In an arid and dry country, the Jordan is a vessel of life. Trees and plants surround it; animals, birds, and fish live and thrive in the environment it offers. To stand on the banks of that river and picture Jesus being baptized by his cousin John the Baptist at some nearby location was awe-inspiring. As we stood there, I remembered that this was another instance of God bestowing blessing when He spoke these words over Jesus: "This is My beloved Son, in whom I am well pleased" (Matthew 3:17 NKJV).

Because we had so recently stood on the banks of the Jordan, it was even more of a stark contrast when our tour bus stopped, not too many miles away, on the shore of another body of water: the Dead Sea. The Jordan River and the Dead Sea are connected. One empties into the other, but aside from that they could not be any more opposite. The Dead Sea is just what it sounds like: dead. There is no significant plantlife on its banks, no fish swim in its water. They can't because the Dead Sea is a container. Water empties into it but never leaves. Several rivers (including the Jordan) pour their water into the Dead Sea, but the water only stagnates and evaporates there, leaving behind such high concentrations of minerals that the deposits left there grow huge salt formations and strangle out all possibility of life.

One body is a conduit, allowing the blessing of life to flow through it. The other is a container, receiving water but not releasing it so that what remains becomes stagnant and lifeless.

Here is the lesson that God brings to Abraham and Sarah in His first contact with their family: *I will bless you to be a blessing. All the people on Earth will be blessed through your family. You are to be a conduit of my blessing.* What God offers them is not intended to stay bottled up within their own family, their own tribe, their own community. God wants them to be open, connected, pouring their blessings into the rest of the world.

There is no way to overstate what a countercultural, shocking idea this would have been at the time, that one family would reach out to bless others. Society in Abraham and Sarah's day was centered around the main unit of the family in ways we have a hard time comprehending, with nuclear families living bonded together in clans and tribes with their relatives. If one clan's interests were threatened, or if someone else competed for its resources, that clan would go to war to protect their own.

The idea that our goal should be to take care of ourselves and our own, even at the expense of others, has outlasted humanity's practice of living in tribes.

Here is God's chosen method to change the world: He will bless this family so that through them blessings will flow out to the rest of the world.

Those looking to protect the interests of their own "tribe" have instigated battles around dinner tables, between gangs, and between world powers. Abraham and Sarah's offspring would later be called the chosen people because of their relationship with God. But when they forget that they are chosen for a purpose, contracted for a specific vocation, they too will miss the point of the outward-focused mission for which God has chosen them. As part of this family line, you and I are destined to struggle with the same kind of choice: Do we keep what is "ours" for our own sake, or do we recognize that all good things come from above—not only to our hands but through them to the hands of others?

Another lesson is found in the fact that God's calling to Abraham and Sarah is both a pull toward something and a push to leave something.

Take another look at Genesis 12:1. What three things does God call Abraham and Sarah to leave?

1. Native country

2. Relatives

3. Father's family

This description of things to leave behind is more than geographic. God is calling them to walk away from a clan that not only is passing down the practice of being self-protective and self-interested but also is likely polytheistic, worshiping false gods and idols. In the same breath God promises them something momentous and asks something challenging of them. They are to leave behind the script that their families have handed them and many of the ways their families have formed them and look to God to teach them a whole new way of living.

Part of the task of "forming" us that our families undertake is to give us an unwritten script. Our script instructs us from a very early age about how to "do" life, from the smallest details to the most complex decisions that we make.

Nothing forces you to reevaluate the script of your family of origin quite like marriage. In the first year of our marriage, I often felt like Jim and I were having a cross-cultural conversation. There were so many new lessons I felt that I was learning related to little things, such as how to load a dishwasher, how to fold towels, how to have a fight, how to plan a vacation—all because we were "formed" by two different families. Marriage often creates a clash of scripts, where two people realize that not only are they not on the same page, but also they are reading two different documents! The questions and conflicts that arise when two families become one can actually provide a great opportunity to examine the assumptions we've grown up with and ask how God wants us to live.

At each stage of life we are given a choice. Sometimes the right choice is to continue living out the script our family has offered us, which is often something to cultivate and hand down to the next generation. But there are also times we can choose to mark out passages or tear out pages that have not been helpful to us and ask God to rewrite and re-form in us the script that He wants us to live by.

How would you describe the unwritten script handed down by your family? What parts of this script do you want to continue living out? What parts might God be calling you to leave behind or rewrite?

To be caring and nurturing, importance of family ?

God promises Abraham and Sarah that this new relationship with Him, this new life separate from the way they have been raised, will be one of tremendous blessing—but it comes with a reminder. *You are blessed for a reason. Through you, my blessings will flow to the entire world.* God's work in their lives and in the generations of their family is not for their sake only but also to create vessels worthy of being called His chosen people—set apart for a purpose, blessed to be a blessing. When God wants to change the world, He starts with a family. It was true then. It's true now. God re-forms our families so that we can be conduits of His blessings.

Counting our blessings is a spiritual discipline each of us should engage in regularly. But taking inventory is only a first step. Looking for places to pour those blessings outward for the sake of others is a necessity if we want to reflect the character of a self-sacrificing God who created us in His image.

Our blessings are designed for distribution, for sharing with others. Anytime we forget that truth, our lives begin to stagnate, to clog up with the residue of our own self-interest.

Today you have a chance not only to begin counting your blessings but also to see if God has marked them with a forwarding address. My prayer is that today the streams of blessing will run freely through you, a conduit of His love.

> God reforms our families so that we can be conduits of His blessings.

Pray About It

Generous and self-giving God, make clear to me the ways that You have blessed me. Open my eyes to see Your mercies that are new in my life every morning. But don't let me stop there. Show me someone in the world around me who needs a blessing today, and help me to be a conduit for You, flowing freely with Your love. Amen.

Act On It

- Make an inventory below of the ways God has blessed you and your family. Make sure to include not only material blessings but also ways that you have been blessed that cannot be seen (your spiritual gifts, talents, wisdom that you've gained, and even struggles you've been through that have given you deeper compassion and insight).

- Now take a moment to pray over each blessing you listed, thanking God and asking how He may want you to use it to bless others. Write the "forwarding address" next to each blessing, and then choose one to act on this week.

Day 3: God of the Desert

Read God's Word

^{1} *Now Sarai, Abram's wife, had borne him no children. But she had an Egyptian slave named Hagar;* ^{2} *so she said to Abram, "The LORD has kept me from having children. Go, sleep with my slave; perhaps I can build a family through her."*

Abram agreed to what Sarai said. ^{3} *So after Abram had been living in Canaan ten years, Sarai his wife took her Egyptian slave Hagar and gave her to her husband to be his wife.* ^{4} *He slept with Hagar, and she conceived.*

When she knew she was pregnant, she began to despise her mistress. ^{5} *Then Sarai said to Abram, "You are responsible for the wrong I am suffering. I put my slave in your arms, and now that she knows she is pregnant, she despises me. May the LORD judge between you and me."*

^{6} *"Your slave is in your hands," Abram said. "Do with her whatever you think best." Then Sarai mistreated Hagar; so she fled from her.*

^{7} *The angel of the LORD found Hagar near a spring in the desert; it was the spring that is beside the road to Shur.* ^{8} *And he said, "Hagar, slave of Sarai, where have you come from, and where are you going?"*

"I'm running away from my mistress Sarai," she answered.

⁹ Then the angel of the LORD told her, "Go back to your mistress and submit to her." ¹⁰ The angel added, "I will increase your descendants so much that they will be too numerous to count."

¹¹ The angel of the LORD also said to her:

"You are now pregnant
    and you will give birth to a son.
You shall name him Ishmael,
    for the LORD has heard of your misery.
¹² He will be a wild donkey of a man;
    his hand will be against everyone
    and everyone's hand against him,
and he will live in hostility
    toward all his brothers."

¹³ She gave this name to the LORD who spoke to her: "You are the God who sees me," for she said, "I have now seen the One who sees me."

Genesis 16:1-13

Reflect and Respond

There's something you notice right away about this family God is calling to change the world: they're not perfect. If God could have chosen the perfect family to be His conduit of blessing, He probably would have. The problem is, there is no such thing as the perfect family. So instead, God chose to use a flawed family, one with imperfections, shining His glory through their cracks to bring light to the world.

Abraham and Sarah's imperfect family includes struggle with inner character weaknesses, difficulties in their relationship, and one major physical obstacle to God's plan: they are childless. Since God has promised that an entire nation would be born through them to bless the world, this presents an immediate and serious barrier. It's a problem for Abraham and Sarah, who are far beyond childbearing years, and it's a problem for us, since we would really like God's presence in our life to be accompanied by an easy road, clear of any obstacles. But it's not a problem for God. God has no trouble working in difficult circumstances. In fact, He seems to enjoy it, using the toughest cases to work out His story in the world.

Abraham and Sarah are a reminder for us that easy circumstances are no proof of God's blessing, and difficult circumstances are no indication of His absence.

> Easy circumstances are no proof of God's blessing, and difficult circumstances are no indication of His absence.

The changing conditions in our lives are not a good barometer for God's power, mercy, or love because God is the only thing we can truly count on not to change.

Abraham and Sarah's challenge is going to get harder before it gets easier, and that's going to require learning a deep trust in a trustworthy God. Such trust is clearly not there yet for Sarah because when God's plan doesn't unfold as quickly as she expects, Sarah decides to make things happen herself.

Reread Genesis 16:2. What is Sarah's plan?

to build a family through Hagar

Sarah's solution involves sending her maid, Hagar, into her husband's bed and taking herself out of the baby-making equation. While this seems scandalous to us, it wasn't unheard of at the time. When Hagar finds herself pregnant, there is a lot of rejoicing; but what happens next shouldn't be too hard to predict.

According to Genesis 16:4, what does Hagar begin to do when she finds out she is pregnant?

She began to dispise Sarai

As Hagar's belly grows, so does her attitude. We can picture how awkward life must be in the home of the expectant trio. Maybe Hagar drops things and asks Sarah to pick them up for her. Maybe she holds her aching back until Sarah feels obliged to clean the floor and let her rest. Maybe Abraham steps in, saying: "Hagar's not feeling well tonight, Sarah. Would you make her a nice dinner." Sarah must burn with irritation and anger, so she begins to retaliate, making Hagar's life miserable.

Despondent, Hagar flees the home that had once been a haven to her and runs away into the desert. There, beside a spring, dejected and alone, she hears the voice of God speaking to her—not to one of God's chosen people but to her, a slave, a foreigner, a runaway.

Reread Genesis 16:8. What does the angel of the Lord say to Hagar?

Go back to Sarai and submit to her.
Where have you come from & where are you going

Out in the desert God sees one frightened slave girl who feels that no one sees her, and God speaks familiar words, words that echo those spoken to His first runaway children in a garden: "Where are you?" (Genesis 3:9). God is always chasing after and looking for His lost children. No matter our status in other people's eyes, each one of us is worth a search and rescue operation to God.

> No matter our status in other people's eyes, each one of us is worth a search and rescue operation to God.

Read Matthew 18:12-14.

In what ways is God compared to a shepherd here?

If one sheep wanders away, he will go search for them

How do these verses reassure us of our worth to God?

God will never leave us, no matter what

When God finds Hagar in the desert, He gives her instructions followed by a promise.

Reread Genesis 16:9-12.

What does God tell Hagar to do? (v. 9)

Go back to her mistress & submit to her

What promise does God make? (v. 10)

increase your descendants

What is she to name her son and why? (v. 11)

Ishmael because the Lord has heard of your misery

Summarize what God tells her about her son. (v. 12)

He'll be wild & live in open hostility

God promises that her son will grow and become the leader of his own nation. His name will be Ishmael, God says, "for the LORD has heard of your misery" (Genesis 16:11b). As God gives her son a name, Hagar gives a name to this God.

Reread Genesis 16:13. What name does Hagar give to God?

You are the God who sees me

The mere knowledge that God sees and hears us when we feel abandoned is always the first step in a journey toward hope. God has seen Hagar. God has heard her misery. God doesn't care if she's a slave or a queen; to Him the only thing that matters is that she's His child and she needs His help.

Hagar is so moved that an insignificant and abandoned slave has significance in the eyes of Almighty God that she dries her eyes and willingly returns home, where she gives birth to a son. She has fulfilled her end of the contract, but her problems have only begun.

When the water in the skin was gone, she cast the child under one of the bushes. Then she went and sat down opposite him a good way off, about the distance of a bowshot; for she said, "Do not let me look on the death of the child." And as she sat opposite him, she lifted up her voice and wept.

Genesis 21:15-16 NRSV

There's not much mentioned about the boy Ishmael's formative years, but the climate in the home they all share can't be easy. There is daddy and mommy and mommy—and baby makes four. There's no real indication that the relationship between Sarah and Hagar gets better. In fact, it seems to get worse when Sarah's own child arrives and Ishmael becomes competition for the new, favored child.

As we learn in Genesis 21, fourteen years later, the alarm finally goes off on Sarah's biological clock, and God miraculously provides the fulfillment of His promise with the long-awaited birth of baby Isaac. We will learn more about how that comes to pass later in the week. What's important today is how Isaac's birth affects Hagar and Ishmael.

I imagine that as Sarah finally cradles her answered prayer in her arms, she can't seem to enjoy the moment. Ishmael and Hagar must be a constant reminder of her mistake and her lack of trust in God's plan. Realizing that having two competing heirs in the same house will never have a good outcome, Sarah acts to protect her own son and schemes a second, terrible plan to erase the effects of her first.

Read Genesis 21:8-10. What is Sarah's plan?

to get Abraham to get rid of Hagar and Ishmael so he can't share their inheritance with Isaac

When she goes to Abraham, Sarah doesn't request this time. She orders, "Get rid of that slave woman and her son, for that woman's son will never share in the inheritance with my son Isaac" (Genesis 21:10). Sarah avoids using their names, depersonalizing the very human outcome of her plan: to cast Hagar and Ishmael back out into the desert where they will surely die without help.

Once again Hagar finds herself wandering into the desert, this time with her teenage son at her side. And this time it's not by her choice. This time there's no home to return to, no family to welcome them back. This time it looks likely that they will both die in the desert.

Read Genesis 21:15-16.

What does Hagar do when the water runs out?

She puts Isaac in the shade of a bush

Why does she leave Ishmael?

she didn't want to watch him die

How far away does she go?

~ 100 yds. away

When things get really bad, Hagar leaves Ishmael in the shade of a bush and walks away from him because she can't stand to watch him die. When she collapses nearby, sobbing, it's not fear for her own life that prompts her crying out but a selfless sense of concern and grief for the child she loves with all her heart.

Hagar is the Bible's first single mother. The struggles she confronts are not so different from those faced by single moms today. She feels abandoned and alone as she shoulders the heavy responsibility of making a life and a future for her son. She would give anything, including her own life, to be sure that he lives.

When God shows up this time, we learn He is not responding to her weeping.

According to Genesis 21:17, to whose cries is God responding?

the boy

Why do you think we are given this piece of information?

to show his love

It is significant that we are told God is responding to Ishmael's cries and not Hagar's because it is a reassurance that as much as Hagar loves Ishmael, God loves him more.

If you've ever felt deep concern for someone you love, you can be assured that you will never out-love God. You will never be alone in your concern for his or her wellbeing. You will never be the one who is truly responsible for this person's future. Hagar's story tells us that when we see and hear the trouble in our loved ones' lives, God sees and hears. And God cares.

Hagar's two journeys into the desert are similar in many ways. They are both times of struggle, depression, and encounter with a saving God. It's significant that the two most vivid encounters with God in her life come in her two most desperate hours. God shows up for Hagar when she needs Him most. But the endings of her two desert journeys are so very different.

Read Genesis 21:18-21, the ending of Hagar's second journey into the desert. What is the primary difference between this ending and the ending of her first desert journey in Genesis 16?

He didn't send them back

God shows up as Hagar's rescuer both times. In her first journey to the desert, He guides her safely back home. But in the second, He makes a home there in the desert for her and her son. Instead of moving them out, God moves in.

And God heard the voice of the boy; and the angel of God called to Hagar from heaven, and said to her, "What troubles you, Hagar? Do not be afraid; for God has heard the voice of the boy where he is." Genesis 21:17 NRSV

Sometimes God rescues you from the desert, and sometimes God moves into the desert with you and makes it bloom. The desert is a place most of us will visit sometime. If you're going through a desert, I pray that you, like Hagar, will experience some of your most vivid encounters with God there.

Easy circumstances are no proof of God's blessing. Difficult ones are no indication of His absence. As you travel in and out of desert seasons, remember that God travels with you. You are never alone. And if you're praying for a loved one who seems to be wandering in a desert of his or her own, it's good to know that God sees, God hears, God cares, and God can make a desert bloom.

Pray About It

Pray this prayer for yourself or for someone you know and love:

God who sees and hears, find me in the desert place. Come and join me in the dry places in my life. Remind me that You see me when I feel invisible, that You hear me when no one else seems to be listening. Reassure me that when I need You the most, You are the closest to me. Wherever I find myself today, make Your home there with me. Amen.

Act On It

- **Are you in a desert time in your life, or is someone you love wandering in a desert of his or her own? Write a prayer below, expressing your needs to God. End by thanking Him for seeing, hearing, and caring. Trust Him to make the desert bloom.**

Day 4: Father Abraham

Read God's Word

[1] *After this, the word of the* LORD *came to Abram in a vision:*

"Do not be afraid, Abram.
I am your shield,
your very great reward."

2 But Abram said, "Sovereign LORD, what can you give me since I remain childless and the one who will inherit my estate is Eliezer of Damascus?" 3 And Abram said, "You have given me no children; so a servant in my household will be my heir."

4 Then the word of the LORD came to him: "This man will not be your heir, but a son who is your own flesh and blood will be your heir." 5 He took him outside and said, "Look up at the sky and count the stars—if indeed you can count them." Then he said to him, "So shall your offspring be."

6 Abram believed the LORD, and he credited it to him as righteousness.

7 He also said to him, "I am the LORD, who brought you out of Ur of the Chaldeans to give you this land to take possession of it."

8 But Abram said, "Sovereign LORD, how can I know that I will gain possession of it?"

9 So the LORD said to him, "Bring me a heifer, a goat and a ram, each three years old, along with a dove and a young pigeon."

10 Abram brought all these to him, cut them in two and arranged the halves opposite each other; the birds, however, he did not cut in half. 11 Then birds of prey came down on the carcasses, but Abram drove them away.

12 As the sun was setting, Abram fell into a deep sleep, and a thick and dreadful darkness came over him. 13 Then the LORD said to him, "Know for certain that for four hundred years your descendants will be strangers in a country not their own and that they will be enslaved and mistreated there. 14 But I will punish the nation they serve as slaves, and afterward they will come out with great possessions. 15 You, however, will go to your ancestors in peace and be buried at a good old age. 16 In the fourth generation your descendants will come back here, for the sin of the Amorites has not yet reached its full measure."

17 When the sun had set and darkness had fallen, a smoking firepot with a blazing torch appeared and passed between the pieces. 18 On that day the LORD made a covenant with Abram….

Genesis 15:1-18

Reflect and Respond

Vacation Bible School was the one time of year we got to yell and run in church. There was story time and snack time and playtime, and then there was my favorite: music time. In the sanctuary—where we normally sat quietly under our parents' watchful eyes on Sundays—we stood in the pews and yelled out the words to the songs. One of the songs we sang was "Father Abraham." As we sang about Father Abraham having many sons, we all enjoyed belting out,

I am one of them, and so are you.
So let's all praise the Lord.

I wasn't sure who Father Abraham was at the time, but it seemed that he must be a wonderful guy. Why else would we sing about him?

That impression was only strengthened in future years as I read New Testament passages that referred to Abraham's gift of great faith. In the New Testament he is mentioned more than any other Old Testament figure except Moses, and the context is usually to praise his outstanding faith in God.

Read these references to Abraham's faith in the New Testament. How would you describe Abraham after reading these verses?

Hebrews 6:15 Patient

Hebrews 11:8 Faithful

James 2:23 a friend of God
Righteous

The more Abraham was mentioned in Sunday school and sermons, the more I got the impression that he was a hero of the faith, someone we are supposed to imitate. That seemed true of other heroes of faith as well.

As I grew up and began to read these Bible stories for myself, I was shocked to discover the truth about my heroes of faith. David was an adulterer; Martha was a worrier; Elijah was depressed; and Naomi was bitter! I was hard-pressed to find a single biblical figure other than Jesus who was a model of moral perfection I would want to copy exactly. He is the only one who qualifies for that role.

While the New Testament verses about Father Abraham all glow with compliments, it turns out his story has its ups and downs too. Like most of us, Abraham's struggles are found in areas of both inaction and action: what he should do, he does not; what he should not do, he does.

Let's consider first Abraham's sin of inaction. As we saw yesterday, Abraham is only a shadowy figure in the background while Sarah orchestrates a scheme that will both create a life and potentially end the lives of that child and his mother—Ishmael and Hagar—by casting them into the desert to die. Abraham seems to have abdicated his role of sharing in the decisions that will affect his family's destiny, saying only to Sarah: "Do with her whatever you think best" (Genesis 16:6). How different the outcome of this story might be if Abraham had expressed himself and stood up to Sarah.

Some of Abraham's other flaws have to do with the actions he takes as his family enters new territory on their journey to God's promised land. Concerned that

Extra Insight
Sometimes the emotional absence or withdrawal of a parent can hurt a family just as much as his or her physical abandonment. Abraham's retreat into the role of silent partner isn't good for his family, and we will see that trait become a family pattern that is passed down to his grandson Jacob, who demonstrates a hands-off parenting style as well.

Sarah's beauty will make him a target for men who will want her for themselves, he instructs her to tell everyone that she is his sister. His faith in God's promise and protection is so weak that he feels the need to not only lie but risk Sarah's chastity in order to save his own life. As it turns out, his fears are well-founded.

Read Genesis 12:14-20.

Who is the first one to be smitten with Sarah's beauty?

Pharoah

What happens to his household when he takes Sarah back to his harem?

The Lord sent terrible plagues upon Pharoah

What does he say to Abraham in verses 18-19?

Why did you say she was your sister, not your wife.

The fact that Pharaoh doesn't have Abraham killed for involving him in this farce is providential. The story is ambiguous about whether Sarah ever consummated her marriage to Pharaoh, but it's clear that this strategy did not work and should not be repeated.

Read Genesis 20:1-18.

This time who does Abraham tell that Sarah is his sister?

King Abimelech of Gerar

How does he learn the truth, and what does he do?

God - doesn't sleep w/ her - returns her to Abraham

What reason does Abraham give for his actions?

He thought this was a Godless place & they would kill him if she was his wife

What happens?

Abimelech gave Abraham some of his sheep, goats, cattle, servants and told him to find a place to live on his land.

Here we find Abraham again passing off Sarah as his sister, this time to Abimelek, who mercifully sends Sarah back to her husband after God warns him in a dream. Abraham, who is called to bring blessing to other nations, has instead brought curses on them because of his fear and dishonesty. Instead of protecting the one closest to him, his wife, he has put his own needs and fears for his life ahead of any real consideration for Sarah. Instead of learning his lesson from the first disastrous false marriage, he repeats his mistakes, manipulating Sarah by telling her, "This is how you can show your love to me: Everywhere we go, say of me, 'He is my brother'" (Genesis 20:13). *Everywhere* they went? How many times did he put Sarah through this ruse?

So this is our figure of great faith? God's choice to father a great nation? The man in whose footsteps we're encouraged again and again in the New Testament to follow? This is Father Abraham that I sang about so joyfully in Bible school?

Abraham doesn't have it all right, but he gets at least one thing right. He has faith in the right God. It's this faith that is highlighted in Genesis 15.

Write Genesis 15:6 below:

> And Abram believed the Lord, and the Lord counted him as righteous because of his faith.

This point is so significant that it is repeated three times in the New Testament, each time in a different context (see Romans 4:3; Galatians 3:6; James 2:23).

Perhaps you're thinking, *But Abraham didn't have enough faith in God's plan to stop his wife from putting her own scheme into action when the waiting got tough, and he didn't have faith that God would protect him in enemy country unless he changed his wife's identity to protect his own hide. Why, then, does the Bible give him so much credit for the strength of his belief in the Lord?* I think the answer is the nature of Abraham's covenant relationship with God.

When we hear the word *covenant*, we may think of it in a religious context, but in Abraham and Sarah's day, it was a word used to describe a contract between two parties. Many ritual practices by which people entered into a covenant required the sacrifice of animals as a way of signing the agreement in blood. In fact, the original language of making a covenant was literally to say that two people had "cut a covenant," signifying that blood had been spilled.

Reread Genesis 15:7-11.

What does God send Abraham to gather? (v. 9)

> a 3 yr. old heifer, female goat, ram, a turtledove, & a young pigeon

What does Abraham proceed to do? (v. 10)

> Killed all and cut them in ½ except the birds

When God gives Abraham a list of specific animals to gather, Abraham seems to know exactly what will happen next. Without any further recorded instructions, he returns with the requested animals and goes about cutting each of them in half. It's a gruesome scene to those of us reading this in modern times, but we have to remember that in Abraham's culture slaughtering your own food before preparing it for the table was a daily reality. They probably didn't blink at this kind of scene, since animal sacrifice was also commonplace. Still, I would venture to say this story will never end up in any children's picture Bible!

In this type of covenant, the two parties entering the agreement walk a ceremonial path between the pieces of the animals.

Read Jeremiah 34:18. According to this description, what would happen to someone who broke a covenant agreement?

You will get apart!

By walking between the pieces of the animals, the parties were essentially saying, "If I violate our agreement, if I abuse your trust in me, this is what you can do to me as punishment. I am willing to be torn limb from limb."

Abraham is obviously ready to walk the path of covenant with God, no matter the gruesome consequences he may face at the heart of their agreement. But something unexpected happens to him.

Reread Genesis 15:12-17.

What happens to Abraham? (v. 12) *He fell into a deep sleep, & a terrifying darkness came down over him.*

What happens next? (v. 17) *Abram saw a smoking firepot & a flaming torch pass between the halves of the carcasses.*

After falling into a deep sleep (not unlike Adam in Genesis 2:21), Abraham sees the vision of a smoking firepot with a blazing torch passing between the halves of the animals. Fire and smoke in the Bible are often symbols of the presence of God.

Look up the following Scriptures. How does each of these passages indicate God's presence with His people?

Exodus 19:18 *All of Mount Sinai was covered with smoke because the Lord had descended on it in the form of fire. The whole mountain shook violently.*

Nehemiah 9:19 *The pillar of cloud led them forward by day and the pillar of fire showed them the way by night.*

> *You in your great mercies did not forsake them in the wilderness; the pillar of cloud that led them in the way did not leave them by day, nor the pillar of fire by night that gave them light on the way by which they should go.*
> Nehemiah 9:19
> NRSV

65

Abraham's sleep involves a "thick and dreadful darkness" (Genesis 15:12) as God describes the hard road ahead for his descendants in slavery. But God is quick to light the darkness with the promise of redemption for Abraham's descendants. Then the firepot and torch pass between the halves of the animals.

As these displays of God's presence move along the ceremonial path, something amazing becomes clear. Instead of asking Abraham to make the covenant walk, *God* makes the covenant walk. God is saying something like this: "I understand that you are human, and that being human means messing up, breaking covenant, hurting yourselves, and hurting me in the process. When you do mess up, I could tear you limb from limb as payback. That is well within my rights as your Creator and your God. You deserve it. But instead of asking you to walk this path of sacrifice, I will walk it myself. I love you that much. I will take the pledge that should be yours, and should this covenant be broken, I will repair it with my own death."

Look up Hebrews 6:13-15. What do these verses say is the thing of greatest value that God could swear by in this agreement?

God took an oath in his own name

This scene is an astounding act of covenant, unlike any other depicted in Scripture. God is promising that when Abraham and his descendants sin and make a mess of things, He will take responsibility for restoring the covenant even if it means paying the price of death Himself.

It's not until God is hanging on a cross that anyone will have a glimpse of how this promise could ever be fulfilled—how it is possible that God Himself could ever die. The prophet Isaiah echoes the prediction of Jesus' suffering on our behalf.

Read Isaiah 53:5 and rewrite the verse in your own words below:

By Christ's death, he promised to make us whole - heals us.

Even though our transgressions are great, our sins of action and inaction deserve punishment, and we break our end of the covenant, God is still holding up His end. In fact, God is keeping both His and ours.

This is what makes Abraham's faith so great that we would read and preach and sing about him for centuries to come:

Abraham's gift is not that he has a perfect faith but that he has a perfect God.

Your faith may seem pretty imperfect on some days. You may fail to do the things you know you should. You may do the things you know you shouldn't. If

> *But he was wounded for our transgressions, crushed for our iniquities; upon him was the punishment that made us whole, and by his bruises we are healed.*
> Isaiah 53:5 NRSV

that's the case, welcome to the family—a family full of perfectly loved children. I am one of them, and so are you. Because of Father Abraham, you can know that your imperfect faith is enough because it is based in our perfect, covenant God.

Pray About It

God, You are the maker and keeper of covenants. When I mess up and don't keep my end of the covenant relationship, You keep both Yours and mine. Even though I don't have perfect faith, thank You that because You are the perfect God, my faith is enough. Amen.

Act On It

• **Fill in the blanks below and reflect on this statement:**

_____Robin_____ 's gift is not that
(your name)

_____Robin_____ has a perfect faith but that
(your name)

_____Robin_____ has a perfect God.
(your name)

Day 5: The Gift

Read God's Word

¹ *Some time later God tested Abraham. He said to him, "Abraham!"*
"Here I am," he replied.
² *Then God said, "Take your son, your only son, whom you love—Isaac—and go to the region of Moriah. Sacrifice him there as a burnt offering on a mountain I will show you."*
³ *Early the next morning Abraham got up and loaded his donkey. He took with him two of his servants and his son Isaac. When he had cut enough wood for the burnt offering, he set out for the place God had told him about.* ⁴ *On the third day Abraham looked up and saw the place in the distance.* ⁵ *He said to his servants, "Stay here with the donkey while I and the boy go over there. We will worship and then we will come back to you."*

⁶ Abraham took the wood for the burnt offering and placed it on his son Isaac, and he himself carried the fire and the knife. As the two of them went on together, ⁷ Isaac spoke up and said to his father Abraham, "Father?"

"Yes, my son?" Abraham replied.

"The fire and wood are here," Isaac said, "but where is the lamb for the burnt offering?"

⁸ Abraham answered, "God himself will provide the lamb for the burnt offering, my son." And the two of them went on together.

⁹ When they reached the place God had told him about, Abraham built an altar there and arranged the wood on it. He bound his son Isaac and laid him on the altar, on top of the wood. ¹⁰ Then he reached out his hand and took the knife to slay his son. But the angel of the LORD called out to him from heaven, "Abraham! Abraham!"

"Here I am," he replied.

¹² "Do not lay a hand on the boy," he said. "Do not do anything to him. Now I know that you fear God, because you have not withheld from me your son, your only son."

¹³ Abraham looked up and there in a thicket he saw a ram caught by its horns. He went over and took the ram and sacrificed it as a burnt offering instead of his son. ¹⁴ So Abraham called that place The LORD Will Provide. And to this day it is said, "On the mountain of the LORD it will be provided."

Genesis 22:1-14

Reflect and Respond

One of the greatest privileges of my role as a pastor is to baptize people, both old and young. Christian baptism has roots in the Jewish practice of circumcision, one that originates with Abraham and Sarah's family as a mark of God's covenant in Genesis 17. Both circumcision and baptism are rites of passage into a family of faith. Because Jews initiated babies as young as eight days old into their faith, some Christian denominations have continued that tradition by baptizing even the youngest of babies, marking their baptism day as a kind of adoption celebration into the family of God.

When I baptize a baby and take that squirming bundle from his or her mother's arms, there's a different picture from Abraham and Sarah's journey that pops into my mind—not a story about circumcision but about sacrifice.

Most of Abraham and Sarah's story is spent waiting, wondering if God will fulfill His promise to give them a child. So when Isaac finally arrives, you'd expect some fanfare. You'd at least think they would pass around some cigars. Instead, Scripture shares the news with these terse words.

Reread Genesis 21:2-5 and write below the details given in these verses:

That's the whole announcement. He was born. They named him. They circumcised him. And Abraham was one hundred years old. There's nothing about the baby. Was he cute? Did he have a full head of hair? How much did he weigh? And how is Sarah doing? Abraham's age at the time is impressive, but a ninety-year-old woman just gave birth! Let's at least mention her!

I've always blamed this lack of information on the conventional history of biblical narrators being, well, male. Men don't often elaborate on stories like this. When my husband, Jim, is the first to get the news that friends have had their baby, he usually says, "They had the baby." Sometimes I even have to prod, "Is it a girl or a boy?" To which Jim usually replies: "I didn't think to ask." The Bible's anticlimactic announcement of Isaac's birth feels like that: "They had the baby."

The truth is that anytime a moment in Scripture feels anticlimactic, it's probably because it's not the climax of the story after all. The emotional pinnacle of this story comes a few chapters later, when the narrator slows the pace down, building up our anticipation with a startling word from God.

Reread Genesis 22:2. What does God ask Abraham to do?

Take Isaac to the land of Moriah and sacrifice him as a burnt offering on one of the mountains.

This story makes most of us very uncomfortable. A father sacrificing his son: unthinkable. A God who would require such heartbreak: unimaginable. It's a scandalous thought. It's certainly not a part of the Bible we would choose to read to our children as a bedtime story!

This is the climactic moment of Abraham and Sarah's story when we find out whether they are going to be able to follow God's will, and Abraham's response will definitely answer that once and for all. So far both Abraham and Sarah have failed miserably in their new vocation of being a blessing to others—even to those within their own household (think Hagar and Ishmael, for example). Now God wants to determine whether they have grown into their calling to bless the entire world.

Reread Genesis 22:1. What does this verse call what God planned to do?

a test

With the arrival of their biggest dream-come-true, Isaac, Abraham and Sarah's questions about God's reliability have been answered, but God has good reason to test their reliability, their faithfulness. With their heart's desire in their arms, who will hold center stage in their lives and decision making? Once the gift is in their arms, will they worship the Giver or begin worshiping the gift?

Even more surprising than God's command is Abraham's immediate and unquestioning response of obedience.

Reread Genesis 22:3. When does Abraham set out to do what God has commanded?

early the next morning

It is likely that Abraham's obedience was Sarah's obedience as well, for we know enough information about her to know that if there had been a scene of her objecting, we probably would have heard about it!

This journey up Mount Moriah with Isaac in tow has to be the longest journey of Abraham's life. There is a lot of time to think. And there is Isaac behind him making his way along the path and following with a child's trustful gait.

Abraham builds an altar at the top. Then, taking Isaac in his arms, he holds the gift close and offers him back to the Giver. Not my will but Yours be done.

This is the moment I think of when children are baptized. At such a beautiful moment, why would such a horrific scene come to mind? It has to do with the look on parents' faces in that moment communicating a single word to that baby: "Please." Please don't squirm or scream or cry. Please don't spit up on the pastor's stole or belch loudly into that microphone. I've stood there many times trying my best to reassure those mothers with my calm smile.

It wasn't until the dark time when Jim and I went through years of infertility and miscarriage that I realized how I longed to stand in the parent's place for once. The babies we lost never had a chance at baptism except in the waters of my womb. They were God's children nevertheless, sent the express route straight back to Him, too early for us to name them or claim their place here in the church that I love. It was hard to hand the dream of those children back to God.

When we finally had our birth announcement moment, I began to comprehend that release is the lifelong vocation of parents. I will spend a lifetime doing what those parents at the altar had been doing with their precious cargo all along: handing my children over to God.

When I became a mommy myself, I finally understood the look in those mothers' eyes at the baptismal rail—and their slight hesitation as they passed babies to me draped in white gowns. In the act of handing them over, they were formally stating what all parents who trust Christ must say: "This is not my child. This is God's child. I will raise this child in faith, but ultimately this child is not mine. This child came from God and someday will return to Him. This is God's child."

When it came time for our children to be baptized, people asked me if I was going to do the baptizing. I was surprised when my own gut reaction produced a vocal "No!" I wanted to claim my only chance to stand on the opposite side of that altar rail. My closest friends in ministry could stand in the place of pastor for that day, but only I could stand in the mother's place. I knew I needed to place my babies into the arms of the church because I needed the reminder of what I had known long before they were born: "This is God's child."

I need the memory of that day to remind me of this every time I'm tempted to plan their lives out for them or control them with my disapproval or direct their future with my worry; every time my priorities and decisions reveal that I worship them, giving God a backseat to the visible gifts I hold in my arms. Every time I want so badly to be god in their lives I need to remember that I officially gave up that job the day I handed them over to the arms of God and the church.

At some point in our lives, all of us will hold someone we love in our arms and in our hearts, and we will be faced with a question: Will you entrust this person to God? Will you be able to trust the Giver with the life of the gift?

Nearly every time I get to the end of Abraham's story, I exhale a sigh of relief. I'm sure my relief is nothing compared to Abraham's.

Reread Genesis 22:9-13. What prevents Abraham from sacrificing his son? What does God provide?

an angel of the Lord called from heaven God provided a ram for sacrifice

God provides the sacrifice just as Abraham promised Isaac He would. In that moment Abraham learns something about this untested God, the God who stands apart from a culture of false gods who do, from time to time, demand the sacrifice of Abraham's neighbors' children.

What does Hosea 6:6 tell us?

God desires love and knowledge of Him

This God, the only True God, loves mercy, not sacrifice. This is not a story about how God wants to take our children from us. He does not. God is the Giver. He is not to be confused with the one who comes to steal and kill and destroy (John 10:10). We don't need to fear this story, thinking that God will take away the things we love the most. In fact, it teaches us the opposite—that God can be trusted with our most precious gifts. They belong to Him first, after all.

You and I have been given precious gifts in our families and in our lives. When we are tempted to worry about our loved ones, to hold them too tightly, to try to play god in their lives, we need to remember that the Giver of all good and perfect gifts loves them far more than we can imagine. This story is a test of God's character as well as Abraham's. It shows us that He can be trusted, that we can open our hands and hold out each of our loved ones in prayer: *This is God's child. Thanks be to God.*

For I desire steadfast love and not sacrifice, the knowledge of God rather than burnt offerings. Hosea 6:6 NRSV

Pray About It

Giver of every good and perfect gift, I am so thankful for the people You've entrusted to me. When I am tempted to worry about them or hold them too tightly, help me to hold them with open hands, always offering them in prayer to You. Amen.

Act On It

- **Who are you prone to worry about, hold too tightly, or try to control, playing god in his or her life? Write a prayer below, entrusting this person into God's hands and giving thanks that God loves him or her far more than you can imagine.**

Week 2
Video Viewer Guide

The Lord had said to Abram, "_____ from your country, your people and

your father's household to the _____ I will show you."

Genesis 12:1 NIV

Eve's legacy (Genesis 3:16)

Desire = to _____, subdue, dominate

"Abram listened to the voice of _____…"

Genesis 16:2 NRSV

If we try to take on God's job description, usually the results are _____.

If our pain is not _____,

it's going to be _____.

"Be _____, and know that I am _____;

    I will be exalted among the nations,

    I will be exalted in the earth."

Psalm 46:10 NIV

Week 3
Isaac and Rebekah

Vanessa prided herself on her spotless home and reputation. In a small community where a favorite pastime was gossiping about other people's families, she made sure that there were only good things to say about her two beautiful, well-behaved daughters. They were always in church on Sunday mornings for worship and Wednesday nights for family activities.

As a teenager, Lauren, the older daughter, began to rebel against her mother's ideas of what it meant to be a proper young lady, and her weekend plans no longer involved church. Still, Vanessa had no idea how far her daughter had strayed from her mother's ideals until she found out that Lauren was pregnant at seventeen.

Vanessa panicked. She was furious with her daughter, but at the same time longed to comfort her and tell her it was all going to be okay. Her conversations with Lauren displayed her fury but failed to communicate the compassion she felt. She insisted that Lauren spend the duration of her pregnancy at the home of an aunt who lived out of state and then give up the baby for adoption.

Lauren refused, insisting that she wanted to keep the baby. The nightly screaming matches between the two had Vanessa's stomach in knots. No one had prepared her for this part of parenting. Finally, the week before Lauren's eighteenth birthday, Vanessa discovered that her daughter had packed her things and left during the night. She didn't leave a note.

For the next two years, Vanessa had no word from Lauren. She felt as though she couldn't show her face in town. Having been part of conversations about families like her own, she knew exactly what others were saying. Depressed and angry with God, Vanessa dropped out of her social circles and stopped going to church. Why, when she had followed all the rules, had such a terrible thing happened in her family? She was no longer sure that she even believed in God.

One night her husband, Wayne, told her that Lauren had contacted him several weeks earlier. He had even visited her in a small apartment in the city where she was making a life with her young daughter. Lauren feared that her mother wouldn't ever consider being part of her life again, but asked her dad to reach out on her behalf.

They met at a restaurant that wasn't nearly as nice as those Vanessa was used to frequenting. She sat nervously watching the door, looking for her little girl to come in. She almost didn't recognize the tall, thin young woman carrying a toddler and a diaper bag when she entered and sat at their table. The fierce tension that had bound Vanessa for so long broke when Lauren introduced Libby to her grandmother. Realizing that her own pride had kept her from being part of this sweet little girl's first year and a half of life, Vanessa wept.

The situation was awkward as Vanessa, Wayne, and Lauren went through the motions of looking at menus, placing an order, and making small talk. But when their food arrived, little Libby lifted her hands out to either side of her high chair and babbled. When Vanessa looked to her daughter for an explanation, Lauren grabbed one of Libby's hands and said to her mother: "Mom, she wants us to pray." As she took her granddaughter's hand in her own for the first time and bowed her head, Vanessa felt the hardness of her heart toward the God she had blamed begin to melt away.

Passing our faith on to the next generation is a difficult task. None of us has the perfect formula to ensure that those we love will come to recognize and claim for themselves the amazing blessings of a relationship with Jesus Christ. Although Abraham and Sarah started a family that was supposed to stay connected to God and His blessings for centuries to come, each generation that followed wasn't always sure how to handle the transmission of that faith. This week we'll begin to learn more about their miracle child, Isaac, and his wife, Rebekah. I hope it will bless you to learn that even as each generation makes their own search for meaning and purpose, God is searching for them. He never tires of finding new ways to connect with His children.

Day 1: What Name Is Given This Child?

Read God's Word

⁹ *About that time, Jesus came from Nazareth of Galilee, and John baptized him in the Jordan River.* ¹⁰ *While he was coming up out of the water, Jesus saw heaven splitting open and the Spirit, like a dove, coming down on him.* ¹¹ *And there was a voice from heaven: "You are my Son, whom I dearly love; in you I find happiness."*

¹² *At once the Spirit forced Jesus out into the wilderness.* ¹³ *He was in the wilderness for forty days, tempted by Satan. He was among the wild animals, and the angels took care of him.*

Mark 1:9-13 CEB

Reflect and Respond

I'm convinced that someday I'll walk into a museum and see a typewriter in a case containing the relics of ancient civilization—right next to the bronze-age weapons and clay jars. My children will probably never see anyone using a type-writer, but I remember visiting my dad's office as a child and seeing the secretary using one to get her work done. It made a "clack-clacking" sound as she hit each key. It was a lot of trouble to correct mistakes, with inventions like correction fluid and correcting tape coming to the rescue. If a document had to be edited, it required starting over from the beginning with a blank sheet of paper. I'm so thankful for the invention of computers, which allow me to edit and re-edit my mistakes!

In the language of typewriters, the "type" is the small metal block with a raised character. When someone strikes a key, the corresponding type strikes the paper, leaving an imprint of ink that bears the reverse image of the typeface.

In biblical interpretation, there is another kind of "type." A type is a thing, person, or event that foreshadows a later thing, person, or event. Biblical typol-ogy is based on the same understanding as the inner workings of a typewriter. Something in Scripture makes a mark on our understanding that has an impact on the way we read a later event. *The Dictionary of Jesus and the Gospels* tells us that typology is based on the word *typos*, "which literally means 'impression,' 'mark' or 'image,' and metaphorically usually means 'example' or 'model.'"[1]

Often as we study Old Testament stories they remind us of things we have learned while studying the New Testament, and vice versa. Many elements in the

Old Testament serve as an example or model—a type—for something that is yet to come in the New Testament. The ties created by these cross-testament echoes help to lace together the two Testaments, reminding us of the big picture of God's story of redeeming love for His people.

There are many Old Testament figures that serve as "types" for Jesus and for the events that would occur surrounding His life, death, and resurrection in the New Testament. Moses, for example, is often seen as a type for Jesus. There are many parallels between the lives of Moses and Jesus.

Moses	Jesus
Evil king killed male babies, endangering his life (Exodus 1:22)	Evil king killed male babies, endangering his life (Matthew 2:16)
His sister, Miriam, helped raise him and became part of his ministry	His mother, Mary (in Hebrew, Miriam), raised him and was part of his ministry
Worked as a shepherd (Exodus 3:1)	Called the Good Shepherd (John 10:11)
Became a prince of Egypt (Exodus 2:10)	Called the Prince of Peace (Isaiah 9:6 and Luke 2:14)
Mission was to redeem Israel from slavery (Exodus 3:7-10)	Mission was to redeem mankind from slavery to sin (Galatians 4:1-7)

The Old Testament is rich with types for Jesus. Perhaps God knew that the importance of Jesus' ministry and our need to grasp who He was and what He came to do would be so great that He gave us as many previews as He could.

Look up these other types of Jesus and His ministry mentioned in Scripture, and list beside each reference the person or thing given as a type for Jesus:

John 2:19-21   The Temple

1 Corinthians 5:7   Passover Lamb

Romans 5:14   Adam

Hebrews 4:14-15   The High Priest

All of these are imperfect examples of what God came to do in our world through His Son, Jesus. Just as there are various methods to correct the mistakes made by human error when using a typewriter, the mistakes made by Old Testament figures are corrected by Jesus in His perfect model and ministry and by His redemption on the cross of all human sins and mistakes.

Why all this talk about typewriters and typology? Today we transition to a new generation of the Genesis family, Isaac and Rebekah, and we will consider an example of typology as we revisit the story of Abraham's near-sacrifice of Isaac when he was a boy. For the first time we will begin to see how God's blessing promised to Abraham and Sarah is passed down from generation to generation.

The image of Abraham standing over the altar with knife raised, poised to plunge it into his son's heart in obedience to God, is one that haunts me. Though we considered this powerful scene last week in the context of Abraham's story, we look at it again today because the dramatic events are obviously part of Isaac's story too. I've always wondered what he felt as he realized his intended role in the sacrifice they had traveled to the mountaintop to offer. What did Isaac say as he looked into his father's eyes, knowing his father was ready to take his life out of obedience to God? What did he feel as Abraham untied him and brought the ram from the brush? And how did their relationship change afterward? Did Isaac sleep with one eye open for a while?

In what ways do you think Abraham and Isaac's relationship might have changed after their mountaintop experience?

Maybe Isaac saw how strong Abraham's faith was in God. I'd be scared that my dad would kill me.

I'm sure Isaac often thought of his boyhood experience on top of Mount Moriah with his father. To unwrap the typology within Isaac's story, let's look back on his experience through the lens of an event that happened many years later—not on a mountaintop but in the Jordan Valley not too far from there.

The scene is Jesus' baptism in the River Jordan. Jesus' baptism looks forward and backward at the same time into significant events in Scripture. Looking forward, it contains significant foreshadowing of what is to come on the cross. Looking backward, Jesus' baptism echoes events of the Genesis story, including Isaac's experience on Mount Moriah. Each of these events serves as a "type" for Jesus' baptism. Let's look at a few of them together, shining the final spotlight on Isaac.

1. The Spirit of God is present over the water: New Creation.

In Mark 1:10 we find this description of Jesus' baptism: "Just as Jesus was coming up out of the water, he saw heaven being torn open and the Spirit descending on him like a dove." The presence of God's Spirit over the water at Jesus' baptism reminds us of the Spirit "hovering over the waters" in Genesis 1:2, when earth's beginnings saw days of a clean and spotless creation. Jesus' ministry on earth is one of bringing New Creation, a chance to start fresh again.

I love how 2 Corinthians 5:17 puts it: "Therefore, if anyone is in Christ, the new creation has come: The old has gone, the new is here!"

How would you express 2 Corinthians 5:17 in your own words?

When you believe in Christ, you are made new. Past mistakes are forgiven. We are changed from the inside

Each one of us can be redeemed and made new in relationship with Christ, but this verse is so much bigger than that. It says, "The new creation has come." This is not just about individuals being renewed; it's also a glimpse of renewal and restoration for the whole world.

Read Matthew 4:1-11.

What is the very next thing that happens after Jesus' baptism?

Jesus was led by the Spirit into the wilderness to be tempted there by the devil for 40 days & 40 nights.

How is this like Adam and Eve's experience in Genesis 3?

The devil tempted them in the garden

How is the outcome of Jesus' temptation different?

Jesus resisted temptation

Jesus' ability to respond to temptation with God's strength and God's Word offers each of us encouragement. With God's presence and the tools of His Spirit and His Word that He offers us, we are not doomed to repeat the mistakes of our ancestors Adam and Eve.

2. The Spirit of God descends like a dove: New Covenant.

At Jesus' baptism, the Spirit not only hovers over the waters but also descends and alights like a dove. In Matthew 3:16 we read: "As soon as Jesus was baptized, he went up out of the water. At that moment heaven was opened, and he saw the Spirit of God descending like a dove and alighting on him."

The image of a dove over water turns our thoughts back to the story of Noah and the end of the great flood. Noah sent out a dove, which returned with an olive

> With God's presence and the tools of His Spirit and His Word that He offers us, we are not doomed to repeat the mistakes of our ancestors Adam and Eve.

branch; then the dove went out again and did not return, signaling the end of the flood. Both the dove and olive branch are biblical symbols of peace, indicating an end to God's wrath in response to humanity's rebellion, which caused the flood.

When Noah's family emerged from the ark, God made a covenant with them, promising to never flood the earth again. God signed the covenant with the symbol of the rainbow (Genesis 9:11-13). This covenant declared that God would not destroy the world because of the sins of humanity.

In Matthew 26:27-28 Jesus promises a new covenant. What is the sign that seals this covenant, and what does it offer to humanity?

His blood, a sacrifice to forgive our sins

Just as the chaotic weather in Noah's story reversed the boundaries formed between water and land in the creation story of Genesis 1, the story of Jesus' baptism offers us a view of God's Spirit ordering the chaos.

3. Laying down the life of a son: New Sacrifice.

Now we come back to the story of Isaac and his father, Abraham, on the mountain. God's call to Abraham in Genesis 22:2 takes our breath away. "Take your son, your only son, whom you love—Isaac—and go to the region of Moriah. Sacrifice him there as a burnt offering on a mountain I will show you." I can't think of a more heart-wrenching or emotionally affecting verse in all the Old Testament.

In the immediate context of the story, we tend to read through Abraham's eyes with our focus on striving to please God by not valuing anything more than Him—not even a beloved son, a promised and long-awaited gift from God Himself. But when we begin reading the New Testament, we discover an even greater purpose for this story.

Read Mark 1:11 and John 3:16. What words in these verses specifically echo the description of Isaac in Genesis 22:2?

God gave his son as a sacrifice for our sins

These verses echo the naming of Isaac as "your only son, whom you love." Mark 1:11 indicates the phrase of blessing and affirmation that God speaks over Jesus at His baptism—a phrase recorded in three of the Gospels: "You are my Son, whom I dearly love." And the well-known portion of John 3:16 calls Jesus God's "one and only Son." These verses help us to see that Isaac is a type for Jesus.

Although God does not ask Abraham to go through with the sacrifice of his son, Isaac's story establishes the type that is realized in the fully completed sacrifice of a Son in Jesus. In an even broader context, the entire sacrificial system

And there was a voice from heaven: "You are my Son, whom I dearly love; in you I find happiness."
Mark 1:11 CEB

of the Old Testament serves as a type for the sacrifice of Jesus on the cross in the New Testament. Whereas each Old Testament sacrifice for sin was incomplete and had to be repeated again and again, Jesus was the final and only sacrifice necessary to cleanse us from sin. Just as Isaac is the long-awaited son promised to Abraham and Sarah, Jesus is the long-awaited Messiah promised to Israel.

Read Genesis 22:6. What does Isaac carry?

The wood

Now read John 19:17. What does Jesus carry?

The cross

In Genesis 22:8, what does Abraham promise Isaac that God will provide?

a sheep for the burnt offering

Take a look at John 1:29. What does John the Baptist call Jesus?

The Lamb of God who takes away the sins of the world

As we look into the types for Jesus in the Old Testament—and specifically in Isaac's story—we see the pieces of a very dim puzzle fitting together. That picture was not fully revealed until Jesus actually arrived on the scene, lifting the veil that hid all the foreshadowing to show us God in the flesh. God knew that we would need plenty of preparation ahead of time in order to be able to recognize His most awesome work in His Son, Jesus. Yet even with all of the pieces revealed throughout Scripture, His people still did not understand or recognize what God was doing when Jesus arrived on the scene as a very different kind of Messiah than they had expected.

Can any of us ever fully understand the amazing gift of Jesus Christ? Probably not, but the many types for Jesus that God prepared for us in the Scriptures remind us that He wants us to get it—to grasp how high and deep and wide His love is for us. My prayer is that our study today will help us to keep our eyes open for these signs of God, and that as we do, we will begin to recognize how much He longs to reach our hearts.

Pray About It

Lord, prepare my heart to recognize the signs of Your love that are sprinkled through time. Help me to begin to grasp how high and deep and wide is Your love for me. It takes my breath away when I realize that the sacrifice You did not require Abraham to finish, You Yourself completed at the cross. How can I ever thank You? Amen.

Extra Insight
All of our efforts to understand the Old Testament should not become a scavenger hunt for clues about Jesus, or we will miss many of the original points made there. But it's important to understand that God spent centuries laying the groundwork for His people to understand His heart and the import of events to come in the life of His Son.

Act on It

- **Think of a time when it became clearer to you what God has done for you through the death of His Son, Jesus, on the cross. What helped to open your eyes?**

- **What response will you offer today?**

Day 2: Matchmaker

Read God's Word

¹ *Abraham was now very old, and the LORD had blessed him in every way.* ² *He said to the senior servant in his household, the one in charge of all that he had, "Put your hand under my thigh.* ³ *I want you to swear by the LORD, the God of heaven and the God of earth, that you will not get a wife for my son from the daughters of the Canaanites, among whom I am living,* ⁴ *but will go to my country and my own relatives and get a wife for my son Isaac."...*

⁷ *"The LORD, the God of heaven, who brought me out of my father's household and my native land and who spoke to me and promised me on oath, saying, 'To your offspring I will give this land'—he will send his angel before you so that you can get a wife for my son from there.* ⁸ *If the woman is unwilling to come back with you, then you will be released from this oath of mine. Only do not take my son back there."* ⁹ *So the servant put his hand under the thigh of his master Abraham and swore an oath to him concerning this matter.*

¹⁰ *Then the servant left, taking with him ten of his master's camels loaded with all kinds of good things from his master. He set out for Aram Naharaim and made his way to the town of Nahor.* ¹¹ *He had the camels kneel down near the well outside the town; it was toward evening, the time the women go out to draw water.*

¹² *Then he prayed, "LORD, God of my master Abraham, make me successful today, and show kindness to my master Abraham.* ¹³ *See, I am standing beside this spring, and the daughters of the townspeople are coming out to draw water.* ¹⁴ *May it be that when I say to a young woman, 'Please let down your jar that I may have a drink,' and she says, 'Drink, and I'll water your camels too'—let her*

be the one you have chosen for your servant Isaac. By this I will know that you have shown kindness to my master."

15 Before he had finished praying, Rebekah came out with her jar on her shoulder. She was the daughter of Bethuel son of Milkah, who was the wife of Abraham's brother Nahor.

Genesis 24:1-4, 7-15

Reflect and Respond

I grew up in a small family of two, an only daughter raised by a single mom. Whenever anyone would insinuate that I came from a "broken home," I felt confused. Nothing about my home seemed broken at all to me. On the contrary, it was happy, content, and filled with love and laughter. My mom did a million things right to bring me up in a way that formed me in God's image and filled me with His blessings. The greatest of those was raising me in the church.

In our small, red-brick church, I felt at home, safe, and loved. My mom sang in the choir, so from about age four I sat "alone" in the congregation—only I was never alone. I sat with a different family each week, choosing my favorite adult seatmates based on how "soft" they were to fall asleep on as a pillow. I'm sure God has a sense of humor, and I wouldn't be surprised if He made me a pastor because of all the times I slept through the sermon in church!

Each of those families became like my own family. Instead of feeling deprived because I lived in a home inhabited by only two people, I felt that I had many places I could call home and many families I could turn to for love and support.

Family is not always a group of people related by blood. Often they are the people we turn to when we need a place of comfort and encouragement. Most of those families from our hometown church are people my mom and I are still close to today. It brings me joy to see them ooh and aah over my children as if they were their own grandchildren. I'm thankful God sometimes gives us wonderful families by the circumstances of our birth but often adds to our kin by bringing people to walk beside us as family we will have a chance to choose for ourselves.

The Bible talks often about our call to embrace orphans and widows, those who are without a typical family structure to support them.

According to Isaiah 1:17 and James 1:27, what are we to do for orphans and widows?

Defend the cause of orphans & fight for the rights of widows

Who are the orphans and widows of our day?

Religion that is pure and undefiled before God, the Father, is this: to care for orphans and widows in their distress, and to keep oneself unstained by the world.

James 1:27 NRSV

Who do you know that needs extra support from the family of God?

We all do

Returning our focus to the next generation of the Genesis family, we find Isaac, the miracle baby born to Sarah and Abraham in their old age, all grown up now but still a bachelor at age forty. This is a detail that apparently concerns Isaac's aging father, Abraham, given his determination in Genesis 24 to find his son a wife. I'm sure Abraham feels some pressure as the sole parent responsible for guiding Isaac's future, since Sarah has already died (see Genesis 23). And the choice of a wife for Isaac is no small decision. The woman Isaac will marry is destined to become the matriarch of a very important lineage, chosen by God to change the world.

Genesis 24, which tells the story of the journey to find a wife for Isaac, is the longest chapter in Genesis. The emphasis on transitioning the spotlight of this story from Abraham to Isaac helps us understand that God's blessing is to be passed down to Isaac and, therefore, to us as well. But in order to move forward in this generational story, we must have a next generation. And in order for that next generation to arrive, we must find a wife for Isaac.

In today's world, parents who are concerned that their young adult children aren't married yet might fret and pray and call them weekly to ask how their social life is going. Abraham has a much more direct alternative: arranged marriage.

Arranged marriage is a foreign concept to us in a culture that prizes individuality and the right to personal choice. Just think about who your parents might have picked for you to marry had it been their choice. Not only does Isaac not get to choose for himself; Abraham is too old to make the trip, so he sends his most trusted servant back to his homeland, five hundred miles away, to find Isaac a wife. Now imagine that it's not your dad picking your spouse but your dad's closest friend or business associate!

The servant in the story is never named, but the Scripture gives us a clue about his identity.

What do we learn about Abraham's servant in Genesis 24:2?

He was his oldest servant

Since it is mentioned that this is Abraham's senior servant—his oldest and most trusted servant—many who study this passage assume that it is Eliezer.[2] Abraham once lamented that since he didn't have a son or heir, his trusted servant Eliezer would be the one who would become his heir, inheriting his property (see Genesis 15:2). That simple fact illustrates just how close this relationship must be, blurring lines between friendship and family.

Those who study families often talk about two components of our family life. "Family of origin" is the family that launches us, the family that lived in our house when we were growing up or gave us our greatest support system. "Family of destination" is the family we enter as adults, the family we marry into or the offspring we have. There is also a third category of family. "Family of choice" is the family that is related by the ties of friendship rather than by blood. These are people with whom we share connections that are chosen rather than inherited. They are the friends who become like family to us. These are people we select for ourselves as those we trust and count on as deeply as we do family itself.

What do Proverbs 17:17 and 18:24 say about this kind of relationship?

A true friend loves at all times & sticks closer to us than our nearest kin

Abraham must have a high degree of confidence and a deep level of trust in his servant to ask him to choose a wife for his son. This man must know Abraham and his values well enough to be able to choose as Abraham would choose.

The word given for "servant" here in Genesis 24:2 may indicate a greater degree of responsibility than we would assume when we hear the word in our modern context. In Abraham's day, someone might refer to the king's "servants" and mean his highest ministers and generals.

If this trusted servant who is like family to Abraham is indeed Eliezer mentioned in Genesis 15:2, he is well-named. Eliezer means "God is help"[3] or "Helper of God."[4] The first part of his name, *el*, is shorthand referring to God: Elohim,[5] The second half comes from the Hebrew verb *ezer*, which means to help or to support.[6] It is the root of the same word given to Eve as a title when God created her as a helpmate. Eliezer, Helper of God, is a fitting name for a servant. This man's heart matches his name. We will see these priorities in action later as he selects a wife for Isaac who has the same kind of servant's heart that he himself displays in helping this family that is so dear to him.

Reread Genesis 24:3. What does Abraham ask his servant to promise him?

Not to let his son marry a local Canaanite woman. Go to my homeland, to my relatives, & find a wife there

Why do you think he makes this request?

When Abraham gives the instructions for matchmaking, he is insistent that Isaac not marry a daughter of the Canaanite clan among whom they are living. Canaanite idol worship is filled with particularly despicable practices. Abraham

85

knows that even though God has called his family to be a blessing to all the other people on earth, including those who practice other religions, it would be unwise for Isaac to marry someone who practices another religion. The temptation to bow to false gods might prove to be too strong, and God wants this family strengthened in their faith generation by generation, not weakened.

Reread Genesis 24:4. What instructions does Abraham give his servant?

Go to his homeland, his relatives to find a wife

Abraham sends his servant back to his homeland to search for a wife for Isaac from his own clan and tribe. There are no further instructions or guidance, and the journey will be a long one; but Abraham encourages his servant.

Reread Genesis 24:7. What assurance does Abraham give his servant?

God promised to give this land to his descendants. God sent an angel ahead of him

From the beginning the servant understands that God's divine guidance will play a big part in the selection of Isaac's wife. And clearly, when he reaches his destination, prayer plays an important role in the fulfillment of his journey.

Reread Genesis 24:12-14. What does the servant pray? What "sign" will help him identify the right girl for Isaac?

For success & show unfailing love to his master

When he finally finds Rebekah, his task is not quite fulfilled. He then has to convince her and gain her family's approval to accompany him on an arduous journey to marry a man she has never met. The servant gives an elaborate speech meant to impress the relatives—but not with his master's wealth or position.

Reread Genesis 24:34-38. What does the servant brag about?

The Lord has greatly blessed his master & he has become a wealthy mans

The servant brags on God's guidance and provision because he wants these relatives to understand that God's hand is at work in their meeting. This might be an arranged marriage, he is saying, but it is truly God who is arranging it.

Bragging is generally seen as a negative trait. According to the following Scriptures, what are we supposed to brag about?

Psalm 44:8

God's glory

2 Corinthians 10:12-18

Only about what has happened within the boundaries of the work God has given us. Hope that our faith will grow

Galatians 6:14

The cross of our Lord Jesus Christ

May I never boast of anything except the cross of our Lord Jesus Christ, by which the world has been crucified to me, and I to the world.
Galatians 6:14
NRSV

No wonder Abraham trusts this servant to find the right wife for Isaac. This man humbly gives praise to God for doing all the work when he could take credit for the long journey or boast in the wealth and power of the master who has sent him. When the servant describes the traits he is looking for in Isaac's future wife, he chooses the same attributes we admire in him: humility and tireless service to others.

If the unknown servant is, in fact, Eliezer mentioned in Genesis 15:2, then this is an even more remarkable journey. It is a beautiful thing for this man, who is supposed to inherit all that Abraham has until little Isaac comes along, to be so dedicated to this family and so deeply invested in Isaac's future. Abraham surely trusts him deeply in order to be confident that he will put Isaac's interests above his own.

Is there someone you would trust to make a decision for you as significant as the one Abraham entrusts to this friend?

Genesis is so wrapped up in one family that it is unusual to find a character who is not related by blood to Abraham and his clan. This relationship between Abraham and his servant shows us a different kind of kinship, one formed through the journey they've been on together and the choice to be as close as family.

I hope that you recognize the people God has placed in your life to be like family to you. They may not have been there since your birth, but you have picked them up along the way like pennies shining on the pavement. Your family of choice is a gift, a precious asset given to you by God for laughter, love, support, and friendship.

Pray About It

Father of Lights, You brighten my life with the gift of people. Thank You for those who have become like family to me. As I treasure them, call me to reach out to others who are lost and left behind by the world. May I choose to be family to someone who needs it today. Amen.

Act On It

- Are there friends who have become like family to you? Who do you consider part of your family of choice? Write their names below. Beside each name, describe how this person has been a blessing in your life. Give thanks for each one.

Day 3: Miss Right

Read God's Word

¹² Then he prayed, "LORD, God of my master Abraham, make me successful today, and show kindness to my master Abraham. ¹³ See, I am standing beside this spring, and the daughters of the townspeople are coming out to draw water. ¹⁴ May it be that when I say to a young woman, 'Please let down your jar that I may have a drink,' and she says, 'Drink, and I'll water your camels too'—let her be the one you have chosen for your servant Isaac. By this I will know that you have shown kindness to my master."

¹⁵ Before he had finished praying, Rebekah came out with her jar on her shoulder. She was the daughter of Bethuel son of Milkah, who was the wife of Abraham's brother Nahor. ¹⁶ The woman was very beautiful, a virgin; no man had ever slept with her. She went down to the spring, filled her jar and came up again.

¹⁷ The servant hurried to meet her and said, "Please give me a little water from your jar."

¹⁸ "Drink, my lord," she said, and quickly lowered the jar to her hands and gave him a drink.

¹⁹ After she had given him a drink, she said, "I'll draw water for your camels too, until they have had enough to drink." ²⁰ So she quickly emptied her jar into the trough, ran back to the well to draw more water, and drew enough for all his camels....

²² When the camels had finished drinking, the man took out a gold nose ring weighing a beka and two gold bracelets weighing ten shekels. ²³ Then he asked, "Whose daughter are you? Please tell me, is there room in your father's house for us to spend the night?"

24 She answered him, "I am the daughter of Bethuel, the son that Milkah bore to Nahor." 25 And she added, "We have plenty of straw and fodder, as well as room for you to spend the night."

26 Then the man bowed down and worshiped the LORD, 27 saying, "Praise be to the LORD, the God of my master Abraham, who has not abandoned his kindness and faithfulness to my master. As for me, the LORD has led me on the journey to the house of my master's relatives."

. . .

54 . . . When they got up the next morning, he said, "Send me on my way to my master."

55 But her brother and her mother replied, "Let the young woman remain with us ten days or so; then you may go."

56 But he said to them, "Do not detain me, now that the LORD has granted success to my journey. Send me on my way so I may go to my master."

57 Then they said, "Let's call the young woman and ask her about it." 58 So they called Rebekah and asked her, "Will you go with this man?"

"I will go," she said.

59 So they sent their sister Rebekah on her way, along with her nurse and Abraham's servant and his men.

Genesis 24:12-20, 22-27, 54-59

Reflect and Respond

When Abraham's servant accepts his mission of finding a wife for Isaac, he takes his orders seriously. He loads ten camels with the supplies to make the five-hundred-mile trip back to Abraham's homeland. Even if the servant travels twenty-five miles a day by camel (almost a full marathon), it will take close to three weeks just to cross the desert. That's quite a road trip!

If there is a positive side to the length of that journey, it is that the servant has a lot of time to think about the important task ahead—about what kind of young woman will be the best match for his master's son and how he will convince her to return to a far-off land with him to marry a man she has never met.

All of that traveling and thinking brings the servant to the right conclusions: that this task calls for wisdom beyond his own, and only God can make the necessary introductions. And so he does the wisest thing he can do at that point: he stops and prays. Upon arrival in Abraham's homeland, the servant stops at a local watering hole and kneels to pray.

Read Philippians 4:6.

What does this verse tell us to do?

always be full of joy in the Lord rejoice

When are we to do this?

always

Is prayer your first stop or last resort, or does it fall somewhere in between?

first

Make a mark on the line below to indicate when you typically stop to pray about a matter:

First stop   **Last resort**

_____

The servant's actions teach us several invaluable lessons for those times when we are struggling with decisions, especially those that are potentially life-changing.

The first lesson is that prayer is always the right starting place. He doesn't go around knocking on door after door like Cinderella's prince carrying the glass slipper, trying his luck until his luck runs out, and he has no choice but to pray. The servant chooses to make prayer his first stop.

The second lesson is that we should pray for God's guidance not only for ourselves but also for the individuals we care for, both family and those who are like family to us. If there are young people in your life that you love, no matter how young, it's never too early to pray for God to guide their future choices, including the person that they will marry. I'm pretty sure it was my ninety-year-old grandmother's fervent prayers that brought my sweet husband into my life. God wants us to pray for the young people we love—not just about finding the right mate, but about all aspects of their future, both large and small.

What does James 5:16 tell us?

Think of a child or young adult whose future you care deeply about. Now fill in the blank with your role (mother, grandmother, aunt, neighbor, teacher, friend):

The prayer of a righteous _____*mother*_____ **is powerful and effective.**

Therefore confess your sins to each other and pray for each other so that you may be healed. The prayer of a righteous person is powerful and effective.
James 5:16

The third lesson the servant teaches us is that we should pray wisely. When he thinks about the type of woman he wants for Isaac, this servant could pray for her to be beautiful or brilliant or gifted or wealthy. Instead, he prays for God to provide a wife for Isaac who is giving and selfless and has a heart to serve (much like the strengths of the servant himself, as we discussed yesterday). The servant knows that these are qualities that will be of lasting benefit to any marriage.

In his prayer, he describes a young woman who will not only do the favor he asks of her (serving him some water from the well) but also will volunteer to bring water for all of his camels, a task that some have calculated might involve hauling 250 gallons of water and taking several hours to complete.[7] (Few exercise routines could beat a workout of that magnitude!) The servant's petition is that God will send Isaac a young woman who is in the habit of going above and beyond for others, who generously shares her time and resources with others.

The day Rebekah's life changes forever is a normal day. She hasn't gone to the well shopping for a new husband. She is simply going about her usual routine of serving her family by getting their daily water supply from the well. Being part of a culture that highly values hospitality, Rebekah responds to the stranger's request for a drink of water because it is kind, welcoming, and the right thing to do. But then she goes far beyond what is asked, doing hours of extra work to provide for the needs of a stranger from a foreign land, someone who likely would never repay her kindness.

Rebekah has no idea that her simple statement, "I will draw water for your camels, too," will change her life forever. She does not know it will lead to a husband, a fortune, a legacy, a place in history, and a place in eternity.

I've listened to single friends daydreaming out loud about the ideal man they would like to marry. As a matter of fact, I did a lot of daydreaming about the same thing when I was single. But Rebekah isn't spending her days preoccupied with looking for the right man. She is too occupied with being the right kind of woman. She is not daydreaming about Mr. Right. She is just being Miss Right with God.

My friend Charlotte was the one among our group of friends who always talked about wanting to get married and have children. When she met David, it seemed like God had answered her prayers. They had been dating for some time, and things were beginning to get serious, so they moved in together. To Charlotte, it seemed like an obvious step toward marriage, but nothing seemed obvious to David. He evaded the topic of matrimony as skillfully as if it were a professional sport.

Charlotte was beginning to feel that this might not be her "happily-ever-after" after all. She called me, asking how to find out God's will for her future marriage. I wasn't sure how to explain that God's will was not only about finding Mr. Right but also about being Miss Right. I searched for a way to gently explain that God's will is just as much about following His ways as it is finding His path. Like my friend Charlotte, many of us reach out to God for guidance on the subject of His will without taking Him up on the lessons of His will that He has already made clear to us in His Word.

I've also listened to married women complain about how they wish their husbands would be more like the ideal man they have pictured in their heads. You know him—the one who regularly gives flowers and compliments and offers to listen to you talk about your day while he cleans the bathrooms, puts the kids to bed, and makes a gourmet meal all at the same time. Too often our focus is on getting the other person to meet our expectations, rather than fulfilling God's expectations for our own behavior. It's always a good idea to work on being the kind of person you'd like to be married to rather than working on changing the other person.

> Rather than trying to get others to measure up to our expectations . . . we should focus on our own behaviors.

The same is true for all of our relationships. Rather than trying to get others to measure up to our expectations, berating them with our words, or trying to manipulate them with our disapproval, we should focus on our own behaviors. After all, there's only one person you can change, and that's yourself. All of our friendships and family relationships would probably improve if we followed Rebekah's example of showering others with kindness.

Rebekah's selfless attitude continues as her family consents to the proposal of marriage and agrees to send her back with the servant. It helps that they realize they are sending her to marry a close relative because her father is Abraham's nephew. What would be a liability today is actually a distinct benefit of this particular match.

Having completed his mission, the servant is anxious to get back home, but Rebekah's family wants her to stay another ten days or so. Clearly they are attached to her and possibly want to throw a banquet in her honor as is the custom. Although theirs is a culture that generally does not value the opinions of women, especially young, unmarried women, her parents actually ask Rebekah what she wants to do.

Reread Genesis 24:57-59, and also read verse 60.

What is Rebekah's response?

She would go

What action does her family take as they send her on her way?

They gave her a blessing as they left.

Remember that blessing is God's posture toward His human children. He blessed them as the very first thing He did after creating them, and there have been many, many instances of His blessing since, both recorded and unrecorded.

It's also a part of God's job description that He passes on to families: we are called to bless those within our family circle.

Has there been a time when you felt that you received a blessing from your family? If so, describe one of those times.

always

Has there been a time when you gave a family member your blessing in some way? If so, describe that experience.

As we close this chapter of the story, we learn that Rebekah makes the same journey that Abraham and Sarah made at the beginning of Genesis 12, possibly even following the same route. She leaves home and family and everything known and heads for what has been promised.

Relationships can also be like a journey with an unknown ending. I often stand before young couples who promise to love each other "for better, for worse, in sickness and in health, for richer and for poorer, as long as we both shall live," and I think to myself, *They have no idea what they're getting themselves into!* The strength of the promise, though, isn't based on knowing what lies ahead. None of us does. Rather, the strength is in knowing the One who will empower you to keep that promise.

The longest chapter in Genesis ends with the caravan of camels pulling into their home camp. On the course of the journey, Rebekah probably asks many questions of Abraham's servant. Based on his description, she may feel like she already knows Isaac well when she first lays eyes on him.

Read Genesis 24:67 and write the verse below:

And Isaac brought Rebekah into his mother Sarah's tent and she became his wife. He loved her deeply, and she was a special comfort to him after the death of his mother.

When we are told that Isaac loves Rebekah, it's the first time romantic love is mentioned in the Bible. Abraham's prayers have been answered, and the next generation is just around the corner.

Where do you turn when you have decisions to make, whether big or small? Is prayer your first stop or your last resort? From Isaac and Rebekah's story, we learn that God is intimately interested in our desires, our needs, and our hopes. God cares about your dreams. As you seek His will, remember that it's not only about finding His path or plan for your life but also about following His ways. Stay close to Him and place your dreams into His hands.

> As you seek [God's] will, remember that it's not only about finding His path or plan for your life but also about following His ways.

Pray About It

Lord God, I lift up to You the decisions that are before me, both big and small. I turn them over to You, knowing that You will guide my steps. Lord, help me take steps to selflessly serve others. Thank You for the example of your Son and His selfless love for me. By Your love I am forever changed. Amen.

Act On It

- Write a letter to a young person in your family or your family of choice. This could be your son or daughter, grandchild, relative, neighbor, or the child of a friend. In the letter, tell this young person some hopes and dreams you have for his or her future. Include thoughts about how faith in God can make a difference in his or her life as well as advice about significant topics such as choosing a spouse or career. Let the young person know that you pray for him or her in these areas. Either send the letter or keep it somewhere you will see it often as a reminder to pray.

Day 4: In a Rut

Read God's Word

[1] Now there was a famine in the land—besides the previous famine in Abraham's time—and Isaac went to Abimelek king of the Philistines in Gerar. [2] The LORD appeared to Isaac and said, "Do not go down to Egypt; live in the land where I tell you to live. [3] Stay in this land for a while, and I will be with you and will bless you. For to you and your descendants I will give all these lands and will confirm the oath I swore to your father Abraham. [4] I will make your descendants as numerous as the stars in the sky and will give them all these lands, and through your offspring all nations on earth will be blessed, [5] because Abraham obeyed me and did everything I required of him, keeping my commands, my decrees and my instructions." [6] So Isaac stayed in Gerar.

[7] When the men of that place asked him about his wife, he said, "She is my sister," because he was afraid to say, "She is my wife." He thought, "The men of this place might kill me on account of Rebekah, because she is beautiful."

8 When Isaac had been there a long time, Abimelek king of the Philistines looked down from a window and saw Isaac caressing his wife Rebekah. 9 So Abimelek summoned Isaac and said, "She is really your wife! Why did you say, 'She is my sister'?"

Isaac answered him, "Because I thought I might lose my life on account of her."

10 Then Abimelek said, "What is this you have done to us? One of the men might well have slept with your wife, and you would have brought guilt upon us."

11 So Abimelek gave orders to all the people: "Anyone who harms this man or his wife shall surely be put to death."…

…

23 From there he went up to Beersheba. 24 That night the LORD appeared to him and said, "I am the God of your father Abraham. Do not be afraid, for I am with you; I will bless you and will increase the number of your descendants for the sake of my servant Abraham."

25 Isaac built an altar there and called on the name of the LORD. There he pitched his tent, and there his servants dug a well.

Genesis 26:1 11, 23-25

Reflect and Respond

My grandfather and his brother had a ranch in a dry part of Texas where they grew little more than scraggly mesquite trees and a few skinny goats. During the summer my second cousin Holly and I visited our grandfathers and got to play on the ranch together. Starting at the tender age of twelve, we were allowed to drive a beat-up old pickup truck around the property with adult supervision. There wasn't really anything for us to run into along the dusty roads, which was a good thing, because steering wasn't my strong suit. I was working hard just to see over the steering wheel! I felt so grown-up, having driven my first truck at age twelve, until I heard my grandfather talking to my dad later. He was trying to justify why he had allowed his son's preteen daughter behind the wheel, saying that it was almost impossible to drive off the path because of the ruts that had been worn deep into the road after years of trucks following the same route.

Like those well-worn ruts on my grandfather's property, our families often develop well-worn patterns over generations that teach us how to navigate our way through life. Sometimes those are helpful and healthy patterns, such as the day-to-day patterns of love and life or the perennial traditions that make each family unique and fun.

Other family patterns aren't nearly as commendable. There are families where abuse weaves a damaging line through generations, or where addiction to alcohol or drugs pops up again and again. Some patterns can be more subtle, such as the way parents deal with money, food, gossip, jealousy, or feelings of rejection. These patterns often trickle down, affecting children in hidden ways. When one way of living is all we've been taught, it's hard to change. It's sometimes easier just to keep "driving in the ruts" that the ones who came before us wore into the path.

Isaac has inherited quite a legacy from his parents. We learn in Genesis 25:5 that he is the sole heir of their estate and the new patriarch of his generation. But for all of his physical inheritance, his spiritual and behavior inheritance seems to have been even greater, an inheritance highlighted in Genesis 26.

When God first appears to Isaac, He gives him instructions about what land he should live in, promises the twin blessings of land and countless offspring, and offers him enough blessing to overflow through his family to the entire world. Sound familiar? It should.

Reread Genesis 26:1 and 4.

What are the conditions when God appears to Isaac? (v. 1)

A famine

How does God measure the number of descendants He says that He will give Isaac? (v. 4)

As numerous as the stars in the sky

Who will be blessed through Isaac? (v. 4)

all nations

How is this similar to the story of his father, Abraham? Look up the following Scriptures and make notes below:

Genesis 12:10

Famine in Canaan forcing Abraham to go to Egypt

Genesis 12:3

All the families on earth will be blessed through him

Genesis 15:5

You will have as many descendants as the stars

Through the parallels in these two stories, God highlights the idea that blessings can be inherited, just like blue eyes or red hair. He wants Isaac (and us!) to know that His promises are not for Abraham alone but for all of his descendants. I'm sure that Isaac is grateful that his parents chose to follow God and taught him to do the same.

> *"I will bless those who bless you, and the one who curses you I will curse; and in you all the families of the earth shall be blessed."*
> Genesis 12:3
> NRSV

We may not inherit a deed or a title labeled "Blessings from God," willed to us by a relative, but the choices our ancestors make can definitely bring blessing to us. A grandmother reads her Bible and prays over her grandchildren daily. A father turns down a promotion at work because it means less time with his kids. A family makes a habit of gathering around a table together for a meal, their conversation becoming sacred space for God to teach and bless not only children but adults as well. The choices we make may be small, but the impact over time will grow with the years like compounding interest on an investment.

"Generational blessing" means that when we follow Christ, the fruit of our faith is a meal that will nourish those we love for years to come.

How have you experienced inherited blessings? What choices made by your family in previous generations have affected the richness of your life?

My parents blessed me, especially my mom was a big influence on me!

In the second part of Isaac's story, we find an inheritance of a different kind. This heritage is the predisposition, based on family history, to make bad choices. Some have even called it "generational sin."

What does Isaac decide to do in Genesis 26:7?

Called his wife his sister

How is this like Abraham's actions in Genesis 12:10-13?

He called his wife his sister

It was before Isaac was born that Abraham passed his wife Sarah off as his sister, not once but twice; but Isaac has probably heard stories told of that dark episode in his family's past. Thankfully, unlike his parents' situation, Isaac's wife, Rebekah, is never compromised by being taken into the harem of another man. But we have to wonder why, after the pain that the past two episodes caused his family, Isaac would repeat his parents' mistakes.

Reread Genesis 26:8-11.

Who finally brings the truth out about Isaac and Rebekah's relationship, preventing Rebekah from being the target of another man's attentions?

Abimelek king of the Philistines

> "Generational blessing" means that when we follow Christ, the fruit of our faith is a meal that will nourish those we love for years to come.

How long has this farce been going on? (v. 8)

a long time

One of my husband's relatives was named John. When he and his wife had a son, whom they also named John, they decided not to call him "Junior" but "Ditto." The humorous nickname stuck, as did his resemblance to his father in many ways.

Many of us have found ourselves in families with generations that might have been labeled "Ditto." Families often repeat patterns of harmful behaviors and beliefs from one generation to the next. Brokenness has a way of spreading its cracks through a family over time, even if we are aware of our family history and try to change. On the lighter side, anyone who has ever said "I sound just like my mother!" knows the power that the way in which we were raised has to creep into our consciousness. On a deeper level, many of us have felt the despair of realizing we want to be different in some way from the generations before us, but we don't really know how to make that happen.

Think of a family you know (perhaps your own) that has seen the damaging effects of brokenness passed through generations. Were there family members who broke from those painful traditions? If so, how do you think they managed to be different?

> Awareness is a huge part of changing the script we were handed by our families.

Awareness is a huge part of changing the script we were handed by our families. The help of a good counselor can be valuable as well. But patterns of sin are not broken just by trying harder or giving it our best. Real, lasting change is achieved through adoption into a new family.

Read Galatians 4:4-7. What do these verses tell us?

God sent Jesus to buy freedom for us, to adopt us as his very own children. God sent the Spirit of his Son into our hearts God has made us his heir.

Mark 14:36 depicts Jesus calling God *Abba*, the Aramaic term of endearment used by children for *Daddy*. It is repeated in the passage we just read in Galatians 4:6. Jesus is the only one in Scripture who calls God *Daddy*, and according to Galatians, we have been given that privilege as well.

When I'm home with the kids in the late afternoon and we hear the garage door open as my husband pulls in, you would think from their reaction that some major celebrity had just landed in a helicopter in our front yard. Both kids just go nuts. The baby, one year old now, starts kicking her legs and bouncing up and down with excitement. Our son, who is three-and-a-half, could be in the middle of playing or eating or even throwing a tantrum, but he stops what he's doing and lights up as he runs to the back door, lifts up his arms, and yells, "Daddy!"

That's the word Jesus gives us for God. We are given the privilege and joy of calling God "Daddy." Now we get to be children not only of our earthly families but of the most high God. Our inheritance is so much more than the riches of possessions; it's also the richness of His character, which gives us an opportunity to grow to be more like Him. First John 3:2 promises that as children of God we will be like Him.

We also receive the amazing inheritance of Jesus' work for us on the cross. That gift means that it's not up to me to conquer my predisposition to sin, whether it is to follow a pattern of sin like my family before me or a temptation all my own. Jesus has already conquered sin on the cross, and that power not only forgives sin but also can take away our inclination to sin (Romans 6:11-14).

In closing I want to touch briefly on a question many people have associated with the concept of generational sin, and that is the question of whether we are somehow going to be punished for the sins of our relatives. In John 9 we read about a blind man that Jesus encountered. The disciples asked Jesus if his blindness was punishment for his parents' sins or his own. Jesus made it clear that the answer was neither. Jesus' actions showed the character of a loving God who came to heal, not inflict.

What, then, are we to make of Deuteronomy 5:9-10?

Read Deuteronomy 5:9-10. What do these verses tell us?

When we read passages like this, our reading of the word *punish* must be tempered by an understanding that the natural consequences of an individual's actions and sin may affect others, including subsequent generations. It is not that God is inflicting punishment; rather, the effects of sin are often borne by those closest to us. Clearly sin has inheritable consequences; it can trickle down a few generations. But what this passage tells us is that grace is far more enduring. Our choice to love God and keep His commandments may be passed down to the thousandth generation. We are, even now, inheriting the blessings of Abraham's choice to worship God—of Isaac's choice too.

Read Genesis 12:8 and Genesis 26:25. What is similar about these two passages? *Abram built an altar and dedicated it to the Lord.*

Isaac built an altar & worshiped the Lord.

You shall not bow down to them or worship them; for I the LORD your God am a jealous God, punishing children for the iniquity of parents, to the third and fourth generation of those who reject me, but showing steadfast love to the thousandth generation of those who love me and keep my commandments. Deuteronomy 5:9-10 NRSV

One of the best family habits we see in both Abraham and Isaac is that of building an altar to worship God regardless of their circumstances—a beautiful heritage passed from father to son.

The truth is that we are formed by the families that raise us, and we are deeply rooted in both their successes and their mistakes. God is giving you a chance to start a new pattern in your generation, to drive out of the ruts that have been set in the past. Thank God today for any ways that He has given you a great heritage in your earthly family. And then give even more thanks for the heritage of Abba Father, the One who so deeply desires to bless you and, through you, a thousand generations of family and friends to come.

> God is giving you a chance to start a new pattern in your generation, to drive out of the ruts that have been set in the past.

Pray About It

God, I'm thankful that Your faithfulness remains from generation to generation (Psalm 100:5). Heal the hurts caused by brokenness that have spread through my family. Make me a new starting point for future generations. Multiply my little blessings and cause them to overflow to the thousandth generation, so that all who come after me will come to know Your great love. Amen.

Act On It

- Think of someone who has had a difficult start in life because of the situation or choices of his or her family. It may or may not be someone you know personally. You also might think of a general part of your community (foster children, at-risk students, adults struggling with addiction, etc.). This week find a way to tangibly bless a person or group of people who need to feel blessings overflowing from the family of God.

Day 5: Isaac's Generation

Read God's Word

[19] This is the account of the family line of Abraham's son Isaac.

Abraham became the father of Isaac, [20] and Isaac was forty years old when he married Rebekah daughter of Bethuel the Aramean from Paddan Aram and sister of Laban the Aramean.

²¹ *Isaac prayed to the L*ORD *on behalf of his wife, because she was child-less. The L*ORD *answered his prayer, and his wife Rebekah became pregnant.* ²² *The babies jostled each other within her, and she said, "Why is this happening to me?" So she went to inquire of the Lord.*

²³ *The L*ORD *said to her,*

> *"Two nations are in your womb,*
>   *and two peoples from within you will be separated;*
> *one people will be stronger than the other,*
>   *and the older will serve the younger."*

Genesis 25:19-23

Reflect and Respond

In the fourth grade I was in a children's musical at church based on the story of Noah and the ark. I wanted to be cast in the leading role of Noah's wife but instead got the part of "Noah's Conscience." My job was to encourage Noah to get moving on the building of the ark, so I danced around him singing, "Don't put off until tomorrow what you can do today" while dressed in snorkeling gear and swim fins to emphasize that the flood was on its way. If you've ever thought about trying to dance in swim fins, I don't recommend it.

Possibly the least interesting song in our little musical production was the one where we sang through the biblical texts that listed the generations in Genesis. In the verses I learned to pronounce names like Methuselah and Arphaxad, while the chorus proclaimed "Begat, begat, begat: It's genealogy! / Begat, begat, begat: It's where it's at!"

Genesis is full of begats. Sometimes these meticulous listings of descendants take up entire chapters with "inspiring" passages like this:

> *These are the generations of Shem: Shem was an hundred years old, and begat Arphaxad two years after the flood:*
> *And Shem lived after he begat Arphaxad five hundred years, and begat sons and daughters.*
> *And Arphaxad lived five and thirty years, and begat Salah:*
> *And Arphaxad lived after he begat Salah four hundred and three years, and begat sons and daughters.*
> *And Salah lived thirty years, and begat Eber:*
> *And Salah lived after he begat Eber four hundred and three years, and begat sons and daughters.*
> *And Eber lived four and thirty years, and begat Peleg.. . .*

Genesis 11:10-16 (KJV)

These passages do not make for the most invigorating reading material. They have been a deterrent to many a person who has tried to read the Bible from cover to cover by beginning in Genesis. But they are definitely more than just filler material for us to skim over. Every verse in the Bible is there for a reason and has a purpose. Besides giving us a complete genealogical history of the clan that draws our interest in this study, these passages also emphasize that family is the central structure of Genesis and one of the essential ideas that help us understand God's relationship with humankind. The "begats" are the connective tissue that ties together both the Book of Genesis and our connections with our ancestry.

How far back can you trace your heritage? Do you know names of relatives two, three, or more generations before you? What else do you know about your ancestors?

Each of the genealogical passages begins with the Hebrew phrase *elleh toledot*, which is often translated "the generations of," as in "These are the generations of Shem."[8] Depending on the context and translation, we might read the same phrase in different ways, such as, "This is the account of" (NIV), "This is the history of" (NLT), or "These are the descendants of" (NRSV).

The *elleh toledot* phrase is used precisely ten times through the Book of Genesis, and it creates a structure for the book, dividing the story into ten sections.

Look up the following Genesis Scriptures and fill in the blanks:

2:4 This is the account of the ___heavens___ **and the** ___earth___ **when they were created**

5:1 This is the written account of ___Adam___ **'s family line.**

6:9 This is the account of ___Noah___ **and his family.**

10:1 This is the account of ___Shem___ **,** ___Ham___ **and** ___Japheth___ **, Noah's sons, who themselves had sons after the flood.**

11:10 This is the account of ___Shem___ **'s family line.**

11:27 This is the account of ___Terah___ **'s family line.**

25:12 This is the account of the family line of Abraham's son ___Ishmael___ **, whom Sarah's slave, Hagar the Egyptian, bore to Abraham.**

25:19 This is the account of the family line of Abraham's son ___Isaac___ .

36:1 This is the account of the family line of ___Esau___ .

37:2 This is the account of ___Jacobs___ 's family line.

Though the first use of the phrase isn't meant to describe generations of people, all ten passages are used to introduce a new beginning, whether to introduce a story (creation of heavens and earth, Noah, Terah, Isaac, Jacob and sons) or to create a heading for a genealogy full of begats (Adam, Shem, Ishmael, Esau).

We tend to categorize generations even today, identifying each by its contributions, struggles, or milestone events.

Choose a particular generation in history and note something for which they are known and remembered—contributions or struggles. For example, a single generation is sometimes characterized by milestone events.

Now describe your own generation. What are its contributions, struggles, and milestone events?

It's interesting to note that although Abraham has a major role in Genesis, it's his father, Terah, who gets the title at the beginning of their section—despite the fact that both Ishmael and Isaac are specifically referred to as Abraham's sons in this section. Isaac, on the other hand, gets his own *elleh toledot* section, even though the generation he and Rebekah represent seems almost minor—sandwiched between the great faith of Abraham and the scheming trickery of Isaac's son Jacob. The two major stories in Isaac's life involve the faith of his father—the story of Abraham's near sacrifice of Isaac and the conflict between his sons over their inheritance (a story we'll explore in more detail next week). Isaac is the best supporting actor in his family, but not the leading man. Nevertheless, he captures a major place in history. God even uses Isaac's name to introduce Himself, a way of telling the world that God's character is rooted in the stories of the people He loves and redeems.

Read Exodus 3:15. What name does God begin using to introduce Himself?

The God of Abraham, the God of ___Isaac___ *and the God of Jacob.*

Isaac's story, although cast in the shadows of the generations around him, serves a purpose, and that purpose is not diminished by the faith that comes before him or the drama that comes after him. In fact, in Isaac's *elleh toledot* passage in Genesis 25, we get a brief glimpse of his concern that there won't even be a generation to follow him.

Isaac and his wife Rebekah, like the generations before and after them, struggle with infertility.

According to Genesis 25:21, what is Isaac's response to the crisis?

Isaac pleaded with God (prayed to)

Perhaps due to his awareness of the way God played a major role in his own parents' struggle to conceive a child, Isaac goes straight to God in prayer and asks for help. Of the three generations of family who struggle with this same issue, Isaac is the only one who simply goes first to God in prayer without trying to control or manipulate.

When Rebekah finally gets pregnant, it is a double blessing: twins! But she becomes concerned when the activity within her womb seems unusually violent—a feeling that must be particularly disturbing since it is her first pregnancy—and she has no medical advice or ultrasound technology to take a peek. So Rebekah consults the only expert available to her, her Creator, to ask what is happening.

Reread Genesis 25:23. What does Rebekah find out?

The two will be separated, one will be stronger than the other, the older will serve the younger.

Rebekah finds out that her fears are unfounded; the babies are fine. She also discovers there are much more serious worries ahead. The struggle is not only about fetuses battling for space or brothers who will spend most of their lives in conflict. The big picture involves a battle brewing between two nations, a far-reaching conflict that goes far beyond gestational discomfort.

How often are our concerns based on our own limited experience and not God's perspective? How often do we miss the larger view because all we can see is our own immediate distress?

Here's another reason to look at the broader view of the Genesis generations *toledot* by *toledot*. Seeing all of Genesis broken down in this way helps us make sense of some of the patterns we see unfolding in the Genesis family.

The word *generation* doesn't refer only to a group of people born around the same time. It also refers to the process of beginning, of generating a new thing. When we pull back for the God's-eye-view of Genesis, we find that the initial story of Genesis is about generation, the creating or generating of something new,

God's ideal world. Very quickly, though, we find that the perfect world begins falling apart, and the theme turns to the degeneration of humanity and their home. Finally, God begins working on the regeneration of His plan, restoring humanity to a right relationship with Him and wholeness within the human family.

Old Testament scholar Victor Hamilton outlines the big picture of Genesis in this way:

Chapters 1–2   Generation (Beginning)
Chapters 3–11   Degeneration (Falling apart)
Chapters 12–50   Regeneration (Restoration)[9]

Generation, degeneration, regeneration. That pattern describes not only the shape of Genesis but many of our lives and families as well.

Check those experiences that you can relate to personally:

Generation:
_✓_ **Starting fresh after a move to a new home or job**
_✓_ **Beginning a new family**
_✓_ **Meeting a new friend**
_✓_ **Finding new hope for today in God's Word**
____ **Other:** _____

Degeneration:
_✓_ **Hurting from the effects of divorce or losing a loved one**
____ **Dealing with the damaging consequences of alcohol or substance abuse in yourself or someone you're close to**
____ **Feeling despondent because of a broken relationship**
____ **Other:** _____

Regeneration:
_✓_ **Finding new hope and new life in Christ**
_✓_ **The moment of realizing that things are going to get better**
_✓_ **The day you decide to start over with God's help**
____ **Reaching out with hope to a broken family or broken world**
____ **Putting the pieces back together**
____ **Other:** _____

What have you learned from the seasons of generation, degeneration, and regeneration in your life?

> *For David, after he had served the purpose of God in his own generation, died, was laid beside his ancestors, and experienced corruption.*
> Acts 13:36 NRSV

Which season would you say you are in today?

No matter what season you find yourself in, God is with you. He has promised to never leave you or forsake you. He has also given you a purpose—a calling to reach the particular era, generation, and family in which He has placed you.

Read Acts 13:36. What did David do before he died?

He had done the will of God in his own generation

You, too, have a purpose to fulfill in your generation. Isaac's name listed among the great stories of his people reminds us that we all have a place in history. Your name may not end up in history books, but you have a unique calling in your generation; and God is cheering you on as you fulfill it.

Do you have a sense of what God's purpose for you is? Consider your purpose in your family as well as your generation.

If you find yourself mired down in life's day-to-day details, be sure to take a step back and examine God's big picture. My prayer is that He will give you new eyes to see your place and your purpose among the generations.

Pray About It

God, show me my calling in my generation. Show me where the world is broken and hurting and how I may be part of its regeneration. Fill me with the desire, energy, time, and gifts to fulfill that calling so that the world may see Your love through me. Amen.

Act On It

- Draw a "life map" on a separate sheet of paper illustrating the points of generation, degeneration, and regeneration in your life or your family's life. It could be a drawing of a chronological timeline or just a listing of major events. Take a step back and ask God to give you new insight into His presence in all of those stages. Share the life map with a friend or with your small group.

Week 3
Video Viewer Guide

"Before he had ___finished___ ___praying___, he saw a young woman named Rebekah coming out with her water jug on her shoulder."

Genesis 24:15 NLT

Rebekah served a stranger. (Genesis 24:16b-21)

Rebekah's service led to reward—a marriage proposal. (Genesis 24:22)

The boys grew up, and Esau became a skillful hunter, a man of the open country, while Jacob was content to stay at home among the tents. Isaac, who had a taste for wild game, loved ___Esau___, but Rebekah loved ___Jacob___.

Genesis 25:27-28 NIV

Favoritism in a family comes out of the mistaken notion that love is a ___limited___ resource.

We don't have to pick and choose where we give our ___love___.

We can ask God to ___help multiply___ our resources for all the needs around us.

"sunset fatigue"- little left over for the ones we love at the end of the day

We can choose to live out of ___scarcity___ or we can choose to live out of ___abundance___.

Unconditional love isn't based on anything we can ___offer___ to God.

It's based on the very fact that we are His ___children___.

John Trent The Blessing

Week 4
Jacob and Esau

Megan remembers a childhood filled with the joy of magical Christmases. The anticipation of seeing all the presents build up under the tree was almost more than she and her brother, Chris, could handle.

On Christmas morning Megan's excitement in opening her own gifts was sometimes diminished when she looked over at her brother opening his. She remembers thinking to herself, *If Chris got* that *and it cost* that *much, how do my gifts measure up?* The atmosphere of comparison wasn't something that started with Megan. Her mom was always extremely careful to point out that neither child was given a treat, gift, or surprise unless the other child could have one too. Instead of making them feel equally cared for, though, the emphasis on fairness heightened their awareness and expectation that they would always be treated exactly the same.

Megan's mom sometimes felt guilty about working outside the home, which complicated things further. When she gave her children gifts she reminded them that the family could only afford nice things because she worked, so, material possessions became justification for her being gone so much of the time. Since Megan sometimes felt that material goods were a sign of her mother's love, comparing her gifts to her brother's meant asking deeper questions about who was more valued.

Soon after Megan and Chris graduated from college, their parents announced that they would be blessing each of their children with a major gift: a new car. Megan remembers that her mom sat them both down on the morning of their car-buying trip and laid down a few rules. These new cars were to be basic models, no "luxury items" included. As Megan's mom put it, "No chrome, no bells and whistles, and no sunroof." Megan and their father would shop together, and Chris and their mother would shop for his car.

Later that afternoon Megan stood in the driveway with her dad looking over her first brand-new car, feeling both pride and gratitude for her parents' generosity. But when Chris and their mom drove up, her heart sank. Chris's new car sported chrome wheels, a high-end sound system, and . . . a sunroof.

Megan found herself with that-little-girl-on-Christmas-morning feeling all over again, equating larger gifts with greater love and feeling as if she had gotten the short end of both. Her mom, seeing Megan's crestfallen look, immediately apologized and explained what a great deal they had been offered on Chris's car. When that didn't soften Megan's disappointment, her mother drove her back to the dealership and traded up so that Megan could have a model of equal value.

Over the next few years Megan began to reflect on the relationships within her family and where her worth came from. The more she thought about it, the more she realized that jealousy always hurt people and never made things right. She resolved not to compare the gifts her parents offered. Megan says, "I came to realize that you don't have to treat us the same in order to treat us equally." Her newfound perspective replaced the tension of constant comparison and gave her a sense of freedom and joy when she was with her family.

This week we will read the story of a family whose practices of favoritism poisoned the relationship between their two sons from the beginning. As twins, Jacob and Esau had a rough start and inherited lots of difficult family dynamics. God's patience and grace becomes even clearer in this generation of the Genesis family, since His love and grace overflow to all—even to the most deceitful family members. As we read the story of a family that withheld acceptance and treated love as though it were a scarce commodity, it becomes even clearer that our heavenly Father lavishes us with the tenderness and affection that we both need and crave.

Day 1: The Rivalry of Siblings

Read God's Word

²¹ *Isaac prayed to the LORD on behalf of his wife, because she was childless. The LORD answered his prayer, and his wife Rebekah became pregnant.* ²² *The babies jostled each other within her, and she said, "Why is this happening to me?" So she went to inquire of the Lord.*
²³ *The LORD said to her,*

"Two nations are in your womb,
and two peoples from within you will be separated;
one people will be stronger than the other,
and the older will serve the younger."

²⁴ *When the time came for her to give birth, there were twin boys in her womb.*
²⁵ *The first to come out was red, and his whole body was like a hairy garment; so they named him Esau.* ²⁶ *After this, his brother came out, with his hand grasping Esau's heel; so he was named Jacob. Isaac was sixty years old when Rebekah gave birth to them.*
²⁷ *The boys grew up, and Esau became a skillful hunter, a man of the open country, while Jacob was content to stay at home among the tents.* ²⁸ *Isaac, who had a taste for wild game, loved Esau, but Rebekah loved Jacob.*

Genesis 25:21-28

Reflect and Respond

I was an only child during my youth, but I was never lonely or bored since I had an active imagination and a wonderful neighborhood of friends I spent lots of time playing with. I always wondered, though, what it would be like to have a brother or sister. I thought it would be almost magical to have a built-in playmate and partner in crime—a brother who would watch over and protect me or a sister who would giggle with me and braid my hair.

Strangely enough, my friends weren't living out this fairy tale of sibling bliss that I had conjured up in my imagination. When I visited their homes, I saw relationships between brothers and sisters that seemed less like an episode of *Little House on the Prairie* and more like *Lord of the Flies*. Because I had no personal experience with siblings, I was always a little confounded by the jealousy and hostility that arose in this most personal of family relationships.

Had I read Genesis, I might have understood. Genesis is especially candid about the bittersweet relationship with our earliest peers, our siblings. From beginning to end, it tells tales of sibling rivalry. As the first siblings, Cain and Abel are the most iconic, setting the stage for the Bible's legacy of "brotherly and sisterly love" with the first episode of fratricide. Then we have brothers Jacob and Esau, first wrestling in the womb and then throughout their lives for dominance and possession of power and inheritance. Sisters Rachel and Leah compete for a husband's love and use their children as collateral in a lifelong rivalry. And finally, Joseph's brothers sell him into slavery to silence his arrogant boasting.

If we ever needed assurance that it's perfectly normal for brothers and sisters to experience strong feelings of both love and hatred toward one another, Genesis offers us proof!

Today we begin the first of two weeks of study that focus on a single generation in Genesis: first two brothers and then two sisters. The ups and downs of their family experiences have much to teach us not only about our own earthly relationships, but also about how God interacts with and blesses families experiencing everyday tension and conflicts.

Jacob and Esau present the most colorful biblical account of a sibling pair. Their early life (starting in utero) is filled with conflict and strife. My husband, with his wry humor, would call Jacob and Esau "womb-mates." They are twins, and as such we might expect them to be similar, but they are different in every way.

Reread Genesis 25:24-26 and describe each brother below:

Firstborn
Name: Esau

Second born
Name: Jacob

Description:
red, hairy

Description:
hand grasping Esau's heel

From the moment of his birth, Jacob is portrayed as a grasping, conniving character. At birth, his chubby, little, newborn hand firmly clutches his older brother's heel, as though Jacob is saying, "Oh, no you don't!" as he tries to stop his twin from being born first. As will be characteristic of their encounters from then on, this is no face-to-face, fair fight but an underhanded, manipulative act of trickery—one that doesn't even work. It does, however, earn Jacob a name. Based on their first view of him, his parents name him Grabby, which in Hebrew translates as Jacob. The name is fitting in more ways than one, since it also refers to a person who deceives or supplants, one who tries to take what is not his.

The origin of their names foretells how different the brothers will be. Jacob's name is symbolic, action-driven, laced with a subversive, hidden meaning. Esau, on the other hand, is named at face value. His name comes from a simple, knee-jerk reaction to his appearance. Quite the unusual baby, Esau is born covered in hair, so his parents name him Hairy (Esau in Hebrew). He is ruddy and red, so his nickname is Edom (Red).

Esau grows up to be a face-value kind of guy. With him, you always know what you are getting. He is ruddy, hairy, outdoorsy and loves to hunt. When he sees something he wants, he simply takes it without the underhanded deception of Jacob.

How can two people who come from the same mix of DNA, share the same womb, and grow up in the same household be so different? That's a question that parents have been asking about their children since the beginning of time. God makes each of us unique from day one, and we can celebrate the fact that God knows and loves each of us as distinct individuals.

How are you both like and different from other members of your family?

Ha!

Read Matthew 10:28-31. How do these verses show you that God knows and values you personally?

God values us + loves us no matter what

As the story of Jacob and Esau develops, we may be tempted to demonize Jacob and feel sorry for Esau as the mistreated and misunderstood brother. But we must remember that no family story is that simple. When you find a family that has a single "problem child" (or adult) who causes trouble for everyone else, it's almost certain that this individual is not the only problem. Families operate as very interdependent systems, and one problem rising to the surface usually means there are additional troubles in the mix. The interconnectedness of family members means that when one family member loses equilibrium, all are affected.

Esau, for example, isn't just an innocent victim as he's often made out to be. He is impulsive and short-sighted. He doesn't value the inheritance that awaits him or his position of authority in the family. Although he is supposed to become the leader of his family, he dishonors his parents' wishes and values.

Read Genesis 26:34-35. What does Esau do that causes his parents grief?

Marries 2 wives that make life miserable for his parents

> Families operate as very interdependent systems, and one problem rising to the surface usually means there are additional troubles in the mix.

Read Genesis 10:15. With whom does the clan of Esau's wives begin? (Hint: He is the first one named.) *Canaan*

According to Genesis 10:6, which of Noah's sons is the patriarch of this line? (Hint: He is the first one named.) *Ham*

Jacob, the assumed villain in the family, probably deserves more of our sympathies than we naturally offer him. By our standards, Jacob is born into a supremely unfair world. The few seconds that separate his birth from his twin brother's mean that he has lost out on the opportunities of a lifetime: leadership, position, and inheritance. The world Jacob and Esau are born into is indifferent to human merit. It does not matter that Jacob is more resourceful, more cunning, and more ambitious. It doesn't even matter that he is more obedient to his parents in matters of marriage and religion. This was a world where the first are first and the last are last, no matter what.

Think of a set of siblings you know well—maybe you and your brothers and/or sisters, your children, or the children of a friend. Have these siblings sometimes felt that they were treated unfairly? If so, what gave them that impression?

Any of us who has felt trapped or stereotyped by the circumstances of our birth will appreciate Jacob's desires (but not his tactics) to better himself and elevate his station in life. Esau's strengths are as plain as the ruddy hair that covers him. Jacob doesn't have the rank or strength of his slightly older but much stronger brother, so he will need to be different. He turns to wit, cunning, and political savvy. But it's the way that he uses them for his own gain, without consideration for his brother, that taints his reputation.

Jacob and Esau are not solely to blame in the family fight we will read about over the next several days. We will see that it is their parents who set the stage for the ongoing competition and conflict that characterizes their sons' lives.

What do we learn from Genesis 25:28?

Isaac loved Esau
Rebecca loved Jacob

Combine the favoritism of both parents, the inequity of the way their culture favors the oldest boy in the family, and the ambition of the youngest in this

113

family, and you have a powder keg of relationships ready to explode. This should make for interesting reading!

I have one caution. We could easily bypass the message of this story of battling brothers, underestimating its meaning. You see, the Genesis lessons about siblings do not apply only to those who are related to us by blood; we must allow the lessons found here to apply to all of the relationships in our lives that God might intend them to reach.

While humankind has always assumed a certain degree of responsibility for those to whom we are related by blood, in the New Testament God reveals a new, broader understanding of family: the church. On one occasion Jesus is told that his mother and brothers are outside waiting for him. (Actually, they have come to take him home because the radical nature of his teachings has given them cause to worry about him.)

He responds:

> *"Who is my mother, and who are my brothers?" Pointing to his disciples, he said, "Here are my mother and my brothers. For whoever does the will of my Father in heaven is my brother and sister and mother."*
>
> Matthew 12:48-50

This is the first time in the Bible that the title "brothers and sisters" is used to refer to anyone who is not related by flesh and blood. In this situation, Jesus' family of choice actually better understands His actions and purpose on earth than does His family of origin.

The next time in the Bible that the phrase "brothers and sisters" is used to refer to anyone who is not related by blood is in the Book of Acts in the story of the birth of the church. Those related by their love for Jesus begin to take responsibility for one another in the same way that blood-related families do.

> In the Book of Acts . . . those related by their love for Jesus begin to take responsibility for one another in the same way that blood-related families do.

The newborn church in Acts begins to refer to one another almost immediately as "brothers and sisters." Look up these four Scriptures where the phrase "brothers and sisters" is used. Draw a line to match each Scripture with the way that the church is acting as a family in that particular passage.

Acts 1:12-17	**Visiting those in need of food and company**
Acts 6:1-4	**Extending hospitality and encouragement**
Acts 11:27-30	**Deciding who will lead the family**
Acts 28:13-15	**Providing help in a time of crisis**

Later this becomes commonplace language, with Paul addressing the believers in the churches he writes to as "brothers and sisters." Even today, many churches have a practice of referring to their fellow members by names such as "Brother Steve" and "Sister Alice."

In all the important relationships of our lives, we sometimes encounter jealousy, competition, resentment, and hurt feelings. We also may experience familial feelings of love, commitment, loyalty, and nurture toward those we are bonded to by our beliefs and our fellowship.

Who in the family of faith have you experienced these kinds of positive or negative feelings toward?

As you continue to read the story of Jacob and Esau and begin to contemplate the results of their feelings for one another, don't limit yourself to thinking about your individual family relationships. God has given you brothers and sisters who are not biological family members and probably have never lived in your home, but who are connected by choice and providence. Be thankful that there is no limit to who might become family to you, perhaps even some members of the group with whom you are studying now!

Pray About It

Lord, for all who are as close as brothers and sisters to me, I give You thanks. If there are broken places in my family, help me to heal them. If there are those who have not received unconditional love from their families and need my care, point them out to me. Help me to be a good sibling in faith to those You have given me to love. Amen.

Act On It

- **What are some of the ways that you demonstrate love to family members who are related to you by blood?**

- **What are some of the ways you demonstrate love to brothers and sisters who are related to you by choice or by faith?**

Day 2: The Birthright

Read God's Word

²⁷ The boys grew up, and Esau became a skillful hunter, a man of the open country, while Jacob was content to stay at home among the tents. ²⁸ Isaac, who had a taste for wild game, loved Esau, but Rebekah loved Jacob.

²⁹ Once when Jacob was cooking some stew, Esau came in from the open country, famished. ³⁰ He said to Jacob, "Quick, let me have some of that red stew! I'm famished!" (That is why he was also called Edom.)

³¹ Jacob replied, "First sell me your birthright."

³² "Look, I am about to die," Esau said. "What good is the birthright to me?"

³³ But Jacob said, "Swear to me first." So he swore an oath to him, selling his birthright to Jacob.

³⁴ Then Jacob gave Esau some bread and some lentil stew. He ate and drank, and then got up and left.

So Esau despised his birthright.

Genesis 25:27-34

Reflect and Respond

In high school, Cassidy and Beth were best friends. They sat together in every class at school and went home and talked on the phone all night. They spent most weekends at one or the other's house. But when they weren't together, it seemed they were always complaining to their parents that the other one had it better. Beth was an only child, and Cassidy had younger siblings, so Cassidy was always telling her parents: "It's not fair! Beth never has to babysit!" Beth would tell her parents: "It's not fair! I have to do all the chores, and Cassidy has brothers and sisters to help her do them." Cassidy would say: "Beth gets more new clothes than I do." Beth would say: "Cassidy gets to stay out later than I do."

It went back and forth like that until finally, both sets of parents were tired of it. So they got together and decided to teach their daughters a lesson. Long before reality TV was invented, they devised a scheme that could've been called "Daughter Swap." For a whole month each girl had to live at the other one's house, do her chores, wear her clothes, and obey the other girl's parents as if they were her own.

When Cassidy and Beth first heard about the plan, they thought it was going to be a great deal. But not even a week into their month of trading places, the parents started hearing that phrase again: "It's not fair!" It's not fair: I never have to do so many chores at home. My parents would never make me ride the bus to school. I never had to go to bed so early at home.

The girls were both grateful to return home at the end of the month. I don't think there was quite as much complaining and comparing between the two after their little experiment was over.

If "comparison is the thief of joy,"[1] as Theodore Roosevelt is said to have observed, then many of us have experienced the joy stolen right from under our noses as we gazed longingly at the blessings of others.

Have you ever compared your life to a friend's—either when you were growing up or in recent years? What was it about this person's life that seemed so appealing? *Yes — siblings, trips*

We might find ourselves sizing up our neighbor's home decor or luxury car or children's accomplishments. But whether we're comparing the size of our bank accounts or our dress size, it somehow diminishes both the object of our comparison and us at the same time. Our neighbor is suddenly reduced from a full person made in the image of God to the sum of the things we envy. Meanwhile we look back to our side of the fence to find that our own blessings suddenly seem small by comparison. Our life, which seemed just fine a few minutes earlier, now feels lackluster and deficient.

Siblings are masters of comparison. Early on, they learn about the mathematical concepts of "greater than" and "less than" by carefully watching out for who has more. His piece of brownie was *greater than* my piece. The time I got to spend in the bathroom was *less than* her time. He's taking up *greater than* his half of the back seat.

Any parent of more than one child has heard the same complaint that Beth's and Cassidy's parents heard so often: "It's not fair!" In order to show them just how much worse it could be, maybe parents should make the story of Jacob and Esau required reading.

We see that Jacob and Esau are born in a time when "not fair" doesn't just mean the oldest gets new clothes and the youngest gets hand-me-downs. It means that the oldest son, the one who happens to be born first, will receive the family birthright, collecting a disproportionately large share of the inheritance and eventually taking his father's place as family patriarch. His position as first-born would, upon the death of his father, make him ruler of the family, including his siblings, a fact recognized from birth.

The birth of twins must have made it even clearer how arbitrary this practice is. The older twin isn't necessarily stronger or smarter or more equipped to lead; he is simply first, even if by only a few seconds. That injustice troubles Jacob from childhood. What is so special about Esau that he should inherit the entire estate? Jacob stares, joyless, at the "greener grass" on Esau's side of the fence. He fumes and plots and waits for the right moment.

His chance finally comes when Esau returns from a long hunting trip empty-handed and exhausted. Esau walks into the kitchen and declares: "I'm starving to death; what's there to eat around here?" It just happens that Jacob, little Grabby, has been cooking something up in more ways than one.

Jacob is eating the last bowl of prepared food in the house, a red stew. Even if there are more ingredients to prepare another batch, this is not the era of "fast food." Esau wants food to eat, and he wants it now. And Jacob is ready and waiting to take advantage of his brother's moment of weakness.

It's not only Jacob who is at fault here, living up to his name's meaning: "Grabby" or "Deceiver." Esau has let himself run on empty so long that he is willing to take part in a bargain that will fill his stomach but empty his future.

We are particularly vulnerable when we are starving, both physically and spiritually. If we let ourselves run on empty, our need to be filled will eventually get us to the point where we don't care what fills us or what it costs. Esau's choice of instant gratification over long-term blessing is one all of us have made from time to time when we have neglected to feed or nurture our souls.

What do these Scriptures say about the feeding and nurturing of our souls?

Psalm 63:1-8

God satisfies more than the richest feast

Matthew 4:4

People do not live by bread alone, every word comes from God

Matthew 5:6

God blesses those who hunger and thirst for justice

John 6:33-35

The true bread of God is the one who comes down from heaven & gives life to the world.

Jacob knows that Esau is hungry and vulnerable. He also knows what he wants for himself, and he goes after it. Jacob has been "stewing" to get what belongs to Esau since their birth. So he introduces the deal that will change both of their lives forever: Esau's birthright for one bowl of stew. Esau agrees and the deal is sealed.

Reread Genesis 25:30. What nickname is forever cast over Esau by this unfortunate agreement? (You may need to refer to a footnote in your Bible.)

Edom (red)

How do you think Esau feels when people call him by this name?

This episode ends with both brothers having what they want but neither of them being truly satisfied. Esau's bowl of food will satisfy for only a time, and he will be hungry again, this time without an inheritance in his pocket. Jacob's newly acquired birthright is the beginning of an underhanded series of events that will cause so much turmoil in the family that he will have to run away, making it impossible for him to enjoy the land, inheritance, and leadership he has seized. Grabbing for the things that look so good on someone else's plate never brings us happiness in the end.

Interestingly, Scripture is silent when it comes to any explicit judgment of Jacob's conniving actions in the story. Instead, it provides a single ruling over Esau's attitude toward his own legacy.

Write the assessment of Esau's character found in Genesis 25:34.

He dispised his birthright

Why the harsh words for Esau, who seems to be the victim of his brother's scheme? First, Esau has always been held up as an example of how a lack of patience and self-control can be ruinous. I like to think of him as the Patron Saint of Delayed Gratification, reminding us to wait for the "not yet" that is so much better than the "now."

Read Hebrews 12:16.

To what does this verse compare Esau's sin of impulsiveness?

immoral or godless

How is the trade that Esau makes—giving up his birthright for a meal—similar to sexual immorality?

In Victor Hamilton's *Genesis* commentary, he writes that Esau's true flaw is the willingness "to put the needs of the immediate moment ahead of any other considerations, to put feeling ahead of conscience, to give away much…and receive back little in return."[2]

See to it that no one becomes like Esau, an immoral and godless person, who sold his birthright for a single meal.
Hebrews 12:16
NRSV

119

Have you ever been tempted in the moment by something that you knew would jeopardize something more important in the long run? If so, what happened?

Spending your time wishing you were someone you are not says you don't trust that God did a good job with you— and that's just not true.

A second reason that the words of Genesis 25:34 are harsh is that Esau rejects what is meant to be his from birth. He scorns the gift that is to be given to him, treating it as if it is worth no more than the price of a bowl of stew. The birthright is both an honor and a responsibility, and he despises it because he wants what his brother has in hand.

Jacob also despises who he is because he wants what his brother has—not what belongs to Esau in the moment, but what he would have in the long run. Jacob despises the connections within his own family, treating his brother as if he is only a means to an end—a vessel for delivering to Jacob the riches he has always longed for. The encounter shows just how little their personal relationship means to Jacob. What Jacob "despises" here is not only the gift of family but also the gift of his own character, trading it for the reputation of one who steps on other people's backs in order to get ahead.

There's a reason that God includes the sin of coveting in His famous top ten. The final commandment of the Ten Commandments spells out for us that it is dangerous to want what others have. It can lead us to sin in other ways and damage our relationships.

Write Exodus 20:17 below:

You must not covet your neighbor's house. You must not covet your neighbor's wife or female servant, ox or donkey, or anything else that belongs to your neighbor.

In our modern context, what would you add to that list? In other words, if God were speaking this commandment to you today, what would He remind you not to covet? Remember to include not only physical possessions but also characteristics, relationships, strengths, and opportunities.

travel, money, house

We are all easily tempted to compare ourselves to others. Don't give away your birthright. God has made you a masterpiece, a unique being. Spending your time wishing you were someone you are not says you don't trust that God did a good job with you—and that's just not true.

One of the best antidotes for comparison is thankfulness. If we are looking at our own gifts from God, it is difficult to have an eye on someone else's. Rather than focusing on what we don't have, God wants us to thank Him daily for the blessings He has placed in our lives.

Note the insights each Scripture offers related to focusing on the blessings in our lives:

Psalm 100:1-5

Shout w/ joy to the Lord – worship w/gladness; Come before him w/ singing

Psalm 107:1

Give thks to the Lord

1 Thessalonians 5:18

Be thankful in all circumstances

Hebrews 13:15

offer a continual sacrifice of praise to God

Give thanks in all circumstances; for this is the will of God in Christ Jesus for you.
1 Thessalonians
5:18 NRSV

What if Jacob had grown up reflecting on the blessings in his own life rather than gazing with envy at his brother's? What if Esau had been taught to value the great honor of his own birthright? Their family story might have turned out very differently.

Instead of the cry of "It's not fair!" God wants us to cry out in praise and thanksgiving to Him for what He has done for us. Don't despise your birthright by wishing God had given you someone else's blessings. Instead look carefully at the gifts found on your own side of the fence. The God of goodness and mercy has showered you with His love. Take time to thank Him today.

Pray About It

God of all mercy, I know that every good and perfect gift comes from You. Thank You for the immense blessings I walk through blindly every day. Open my eyes so that I can give You the thanks and praise You deserve. When my gaze begins to wander to what others have, guide my eyes back to You and give me the strength to praise You in all things. Amen.

Act On It

- List below the things that feed and nurture your soul. Circle one item on your list that you have neglected recently, and commit to renew the practice this week.

- Do you tend to cry "It's not fair!" or "Thank you, God!" more often? Begin the habit of keeping a gratitude list, looking for the special blessings of each day. When you find yourself tempted to cry "It's not fair!" read your gratitude list and give thanks to God instead. Write your first list below:

Day 3: Brokenness and the Blessing?

Read God's Word

[1] When Isaac was old and his eyes were so weak that he could no longer see, he called for Esau his older son and said to him, "My son."

"Here I am," he answered.

[2] Isaac said, "I am now an old man and don't know the day of my death. [3] Now then, get your equipment—your quiver and bow—and go out to the open country to hunt some wild game for me. [4] Prepare me the kind of tasty food I like and bring it to me to eat, so that I may give you my blessing before I die."

[5] Now Rebekah was listening as Isaac spoke to his son Esau. When Esau left for the open country to hunt game and bring it back, [6] Rebekah said to her son Jacob, "Look, I overheard your father say to your brother Esau, [7] 'Bring me some game and prepare me some tasty food to eat, so that I may give you my blessing in the presence of the LORD before I die.' [8] Now, my son, listen carefully and do what I tell you: [9] Go out to the flock and bring me two choice young goats, so I can prepare some tasty food for your father, just the way he likes it. [10] Then take it to your father to eat, so that he may give you his blessing before he dies."

¹¹ *Jacob said to Rebekah his mother, "But my brother Esau is a hairy man while I have smooth skin.* ¹² *What if my father touches me? I would appear to be tricking him and would bring down a curse on myself rather than a blessing."*

¹³ *His mother said to him, "My son, let the curse fall on me. Just do what I say; go and get them for me."*

¹⁴ *So he went and got them and brought them to his mother, and she prepared some tasty food, just the way his father liked it.* ¹⁵ *Then Rebekah took the best clothes of Esau her older son, which she had in the house, and put them on her younger son Jacob.* ¹⁶ *She also covered his hands and the smooth part of his neck with the goatskins.* ¹⁷ *Then she handed to her son Jacob the tasty food and the bread she had made.*

¹⁸ *He went to his father and said, "My father."*

"Yes, my son," he answered. "Who is it?"

¹⁹ *Jacob said to his father, "I am Esau your firstborn. I have done as you told me. Please sit up and eat some of my game, so that you may give me your blessing."*

²⁰ *Isaac asked his son, "How did you find it so quickly, my son?"*

"The LORD your God gave me success," he replied.

²¹ *Then Isaac said to Jacob, "Come near so I can touch you, my son, to know whether you really are my son Esau or not."*

²² *Jacob went close to his father Isaac, who touched him and said, "The voice is the voice of Jacob, but the hands are the hands of Esau."* ²³ *He did not recognize him, for his hands were hairy like those of his brother Esau; so he proceeded to bless him.* ²⁴ *"Are you really my son Esau?" he asked.*

"I am," he replied.

²⁵ *Then he said, "My son, bring me some of your game to eat, so that I may give you my blessing."*

Jacob brought it to him and he ate; and he brought some wine and he drank. ²⁶ *Then his father Isaac said to him, "Come here, my son, and kiss me."*

²⁷ *So he went to him and kissed him. When Isaac caught the smell of his clothes, he blessed him.*

Genesis 27:1-27

Reflect and Respond

Broken families don't always look broken from the outside. If you or I lived down the street from Isaac and Rebekah's family, we might think of them as "that sweet couple and their twin boys." But inside their house things are falling apart. Even something as endearing as a father's blessing of his son becomes an all-out family war with everyone choosing sides.

Jacob has already shown that he will do anything to get ahead of his brother, Esau. It began at birth with a tiny hand grasping a heel and continued as Jacob played "Let's Make a Deal" with a bowl of stew and Esau's birthright. But Jacob will not rest until he has taken everything, including his brother's blessing as well.

This blessing is a serious commodity passed from a father on his deathbed to his eldest son, with serious spiritual and material significance. Materially, the blessing is just as crucial as the birthright since it is "considered to be the act formally acknowledging the firstborn as the principal heir."[3] This moment of blessing is like the signing of a will, where the father states his personal wishes that this oldest son will inherit and rule the estate. The spiritual significance of the blessing means that God's special relationship with this family is handed down through the generations.

Read Genesis 17:7. What is God's promise, and for whom is it intended?

God, us, & our offspring
To be God to us & our offspring.

This entire family will be God's people, walking through life accompanied by God's presence. The original promise of God's presence to Abraham is far greater than any promise of rich land or countless offspring.

Parents today still feel the challenge of handing down their faith to the next generation. Faithful parents try their best to give their children a strong foundation of faith as they teach and pray with them at home and raise them as a part of a church family. In the end, though, children must decide for themselves what they will believe and whom they will worship. God has no "grandchildren," so the blessing must be renewed by a decision made in each generation.

What do you think are some of the best ways to help children develop their own strong relationship with God?

Take them to church, show them God through you, pray   Lead by example

If this family wants their children to develop a passion for God and for following His commands, their techniques need some work. In two short generations after Abraham, who is known for his faithfulness to God, we see the deceptiveness and favoritism of Rebekah and Isaac, and then the deception of Jacob, who is best known for living up to his name: Deceiver.

In Genesis 27, we find Jacob stooping to his lowest point. When he swiped Esau's birthright, he at least met his brother face-to-face and got his consent, no matter how underhanded his dealings were. In the story of the blessing, however, Jacob deceives his own elderly and dying father by dressing up as his brother. He

I will establish my covenant between me and you, and your offspring after you throughout their generations, for an everlasting covenant, to be God to you and to your offspring after you.
Genesis 17:7
NRSV

lies not once but multiple times, claiming to be Esau. He even invokes the name of God.

Reread Genesis 27:20. Why do you think Jacob includes God in this lie?

To explain why he killed the animal so fast.

Jacob strengthens his story of deception by saying that God has given him success. Yet despite all of his scheming, Jacob does not act alone.

Reread Genesis 27:5-10. Who is the true instigator of the deception in this story?

His mother, Rebekah

Rebekah, Jacob's mother, is the one who overhears the conversation when Isaac asks Esau to go hunting for game and prepare his favorite dish. She is the one who conceives the plan and convinces Jacob. And she is the one who literally dresses him, covering him in his brother's clothes and the hide of an animal to give him the feel of his hairy brother, Esau.

What is another instance in Scripture when a parent dresses children in animal skins? See Genesis 3:21 for the answer.

God made clothing from animal skins for Adam & Eve.

Rebekah sends her son as a virtual wolf in sheep's clothing to deceive his own blind, dying father. She dresses Jacob in the skin of an innocent animal in order to facilitate his sin. God covers His first children with the hide of an animal to cover their shame after their sin is confessed.

Rebekah sends her son off on an errand of deception, one that will end with him running away from the consequences of his sin and ending up far away from her. God dresses His children with grace in order to welcome them home into His presence.

If Rebekah wants to give her son a better life, she should first take a closer look at the integrity of her own life. "Do as I say, not as I do" is not an effective parenting tool. The greatest instrument that parents can use to teach children about a life of faithfulness to God is living a life of faithfulness before them.

Rebekah is aware of the tumultuous relationship between her two sons, which started at a very early stage. Remember that during her pregnancy with the twins, she cried out to God to find out why there was such turmoil within her.

125

What answer did God give her in Genesis 25:23?

The sons will become 2 nations. They will be rivals one nation will be stronger than the other. The older son will serve the younger.

How you feel about Rebekah's actions may hinge on what you think this message from God meant for her and her sons. Did God want the older to serve the younger in a reversal of fortunes? Or was God simply making a statement, foretelling what would inevitably happen? In revealing His knowledge of the future, was God being predictive or prescriptive?

Whether God was telling Rebekah the outcome that He desired for her sons or just stating the facts without judgment, Rebekah's manipulation of the twins' destinies creates immense pain for every member of this family. Perhaps she believes that she is fulfilling God's design by placing her younger son ahead of the older. But God does not need our help in furthering His plans by hurting other people. He doesn't want us to be unkind or deceitful as we work toward realizing "His kingdom come and His will be done" on earth. Sometimes we need a reminder that God's will is not only the future outcome that He seeks but also the guidelines He provides for our present actions and character. As we dream of and work toward God's will being done, we also must be careful to act according to His will in our daily lives.

Do you tend to think more often of God's will as a future event or a present act? Why?

If we saw this chapter dramatized, set on the stage as a short play with a small cast of four, one of the first things we would notice is that there are never more than two characters on stage at the same time. First there are Isaac and Esau, then Rebekah and Jacob, then Jacob and Isaac, and finally Isaac and Esau again. There is even an almost comical moment in verse 30 where "Jacob had scarcely left his father's presence" when Esau comes in to receive his blessing. We can almost see Jacob sneaking out one door as Esau enters the other.

This family never seems to sit down in the same room, talk things out, or share their dreams and plans with one another. Instead, they work behind each other's backs. Isaac tells only Esau that he wants to bless him, but Rebekah overhears the conversation. She then whispers her plan to Jacob alone, confiding and conniving.

We remember from Day 1 of this week that each parent shows favoritism toward one of the two sons. By choosing to bless one child instead of both, they bring curses on the family relationships. Isaac's favoritism of Esau sours his wife and younger son toward him to the point that they are willing to deceive him on his deathbed. Rebekah's manipulation to win success for her favorite son means that she will lose the trust of one son and the company of the other when he has to flee because of his mother's schemes.

Reread Genesis 27:11-13.

What is Jacob afraid of here?

He would be recognized since he wasn't hairy, like Esau.

What does Rebekah offer to do for him?

To let the curse fall on her

Do you think she is able to follow through and deliver what she has offered?

probably not.

We each have at least one person in our lives that we want to see thrive and become his or her best. We may be tempted at times to put others down through our words or our actions in order to see our loved one succeed. In fact, there are things we would never do in order to promote or defend ourselves that we will do to promote or defend those closest to us. Along with the gift of great love comes the danger of great temptation.

When have you gone to great lengths to promote or defend a loved one?

Did this experience cause you to compromise your integrity in any way, or was it an opportunity for you to demonstrate the love and character of Christ?

One of the greatest blessings you can give to those you love is the example of your own integrity. The closer you draw to God through prayer, study, and the accountability of Christian community, the more you will begin to become more like Him in both love and character. Those closest to you will benefit greatly from the blessing of your increasing Christ-likeness. And that is a blessing that can never be stolen.

> One of the greatest blessings you can give to those you love is the example of your own integrity.

127

God, I lift up those I love to You. Help me to trust You with their care so that great love will lead me to do great good on their behalf. Thank You for those You have placed around me who are of great character and integrity. Help me look to them for wisdom even as I look to You in order to be all I need for those I love. Amen.

Act On It

• Look for ways today to give your loved ones the blessing of your character. Imitate Christ in everything you say and do. When making decisions, ask yourself, "How would Jesus respond in this situation?"

Day 4: Bountiful Blessing

Read God's Word

[27] *So [Jacob] went to him and kissed him. When Isaac caught the smell of his clothes, he blessed him and said,*

> *"Ah, the smell of my son*
> *is like the smell of a field*
> *that the LORD has blessed.*
> [28] *May God give you heaven's dew*
> *and earth's richness—*
> *an abundance of grain and new wine.*
> [29] *May nations serve you*
> *and peoples bow down to you.*
> *Be lord over your brothers,*
> *and may the sons of your mother bow down to you.*
> *May those who curse you be cursed*
> *and those who bless you be blessed."*

[30] *After Isaac finished blessing him, and Jacob had scarcely left his father's presence, his brother Esau came in from hunting.* [31] *He too prepared some tasty food and brought it to his father. Then he said to him, "My father, please sit up and eat some of my game, so that you may give me your blessing."*
[32] *His father Isaac asked him, "Who are you?"*

"I am your son," he answered, "your firstborn, Esau."

33 Isaac trembled violently and said, "Who was it, then, that hunted game and brought it to me? I ate it just before you came and I blessed him—and indeed he will be blessed!"

34 When Esau heard his father's words, he burst out with a loud and bitter cry and said to his father, "Bless me—me too, my father!"

35 But he said, "Your brother came deceitfully and took your blessing."

36 Esau said, "Isn't he rightly named Jacob? This is the second time he has taken advantage of me: He took my birthright, and now he's taken my blessing!" Then he asked, "Haven't you reserved any blessing for me?"

37 Isaac answered Esau, "I have made him lord over you and have made all his relatives his servants, and I have sustained him with grain and new wine. So what can I possibly do for you, my son?"

38 Esau said to his father, "Do you have only one blessing, my father? Bless me too, my father!" Then Esau wept aloud.

Genesis 27:27-38

Reflect and Respond

With all the commotion surrounding Jacob's swindling his brother Esau out of his birthright, it's almost surprising that the story records no backlash for that divisive action. Esau doesn't protest or complain. The boys' parents don't enter the scene to scold Jacob or try to reverse the situation. But when the blessing is stolen from its rightful owner, the drama in the story really heats up.

Giving a "blessing" may seem to us like a mostly ceremonial and empty act. We may ask someone to say "a quick blessing" over a meal before we start eating. Or we may wish someone "blessings and best wishes" on a congratulatory greeting card without giving a second thought to what we're really saying. But it is clear that in this culture and specifically for this family, the blessing is a very serious and valuable commodity.

How do we know from the context of these verses that the blessing is such a powerful gift to give and receive? First, Rebekah willingly manipulates her entire family and risks the relationships she values most so that her favorite son will receive the blessing. Isaac trembles violently when he begins to realize that he has given his blessing to the wrong son. And poor Esau's response is heartbreaking.

Reread Genesis 27:34. What is Esau's response—actions and words—when he finds out that there is no blessing left for him?

He wept

What is it that breaks Esau's heart? The fact that he has been denied his father's blessing.

Walter Brueggeman says that "this family of Genesis is preoccupied with blessing, as though it matters more than things visible."[4] Their preoccupation is based on their understanding of blessing as an incredibly powerful and meaningful act. They grasp what you and I should note: God wants us to give and receive meaningful blessings as part of our most significant relationships.

There are major differences between our understanding of blessing and the way we see this Genesis family practicing the tradition of blessing the eldest son. For them, the blessing can only reside with one individual in a generation at a time, and so it is transmitted on just one rare occasion—the deathbed of the father, the family patriarch. It also is a limited commodity, reserved for only the oldest son. Although Esau weeps and begs for his own blessing, Jacob has little to offer him. Clearly the true blessing already has been spent.

The good news for us is that blessings are not a limited resource. Our blessings are not reserved for one occasion or for one individual. We can offer blessing to every person who is dear to us, and we don't have to wait until our deathbed to do so.

There are some aspects of blessing that are timeless—features of blessing that are consistent throughout generations. Our ability to understand and offer blessing will be richer as we explore the following characteristics of blessing:

1. Blessing teaches us that the spoken word has power.

In the very first verses of the Bible, this is made clear in God's act of speaking things into being. God could have chosen to create by many other means, but He chose to create with His words. While we don't have the power to create light by speaking "Let there be light" (believe me, when my son first heard the creation story, he tried!), our words do have power. In Isaac and Rebekah's family, the name "Deceiver" is spoken over their younger son, Jacob, enough times that he begins to act out the words that name him. Positive words, when spoken over those we love, can also have the lasting effect of shaping character.

What words spoken over you while you were growing up shaped you?

2. Blessing starts with God.

God's posture toward His children is one of blessing.

> God wants us to give and receive meaningful blesings as part of our most significant relationships.

According to Genesis 1:28, what is God's first act toward human beings when He creates them?

He blessed them

Read Genesis 9:1. When Noah and his family emerge from the ark, what does God do?

Blessed them

What does Romans 8:28 say is God's goal for those who love Him?

all things work together for good

God cannot resist a chance to bless His children. He is, even now, blessing you. God's blessings don't always come in the form we're looking for or expecting, but Scripture teaches us that God is for us. He wants the best for us and is working for our good. God shows us that blessing is very clearly others-centered, not self-centered—always given with the good of the one who is blessed in mind and with no expectation of receiving anything in return.

Read these examples of blessing given by one person to another. Draw a line to connect each Scripture with the relationship behind the blessing described.

Song of Songs 4:1-8   the Lord and His children

Proverbs 3:1-4   lovers

Numbers 6:22-27   my son [or child]

3. Blessing is intergenerational.

All of us have a deep longing to receive a blessing from our parents—to feel that we are loved, valued, and appreciated for who we are. God crafted the parent-child relationship so that parents and children have a deep stake in each other's emotional well-being. Parents offer children the blessing of starting their life with unconditional love, but children are also a blessing to parents, providing them with a deep feeling of fulfillment and purpose.

We know that all things work together for good for those who love God, who are called according to his purpose.
Romans 8:28
NRSV

What does each of these Scriptures tell you about intergenerational blessing?

Deuteronomy 6:6-9

Repeat them again & again to your children.

Psalm 127:3-5

Proverbs 23:24

father of godly children has cause for joa

Proverbs 31:28

> Blessing is not about passing down material goods; it is about passing on the love God has given us.

Blessing is not about passing down material goods; it is about passing on the love God has given us. We can bless someone without buying or wrapping anything. We don't need a special occasion to bless those we love. Any time is a good time to pass along a blessing to those God has placed in our lives.

Do you know anyone who has received a wonderful blessing from someone in her or his family? If so, in what way?

Do you know someone who did not receive the blessing of someone in her or his past? How did it affect this person?

4. Blessing is contagious.

Central to the call from God that Abraham and Sarah received was the message that they and their family were blessed to be a blessing (Genesis 12:1-2). God's blessings are free-flowing and abundant; they are meant to be shared. Even in the Genesis family, when the oldest son received a blessing from his father, he must have been aware that someday he would be sitting where his father sat, transmitting that blessing to the next generation. Blessings that we receive, whether material or spiritual, are meant to overflow onto the people around us. When we bless others, we become an instrument of God's love, a part of His stream of blessing flowing through us to others on earth.

How can you be contagious with your blessings, sharing them with others?

Unlike the heartbreak we witness Esau experiencing, we never have to wonder if there is enough blessing to go around. Unlike Jacob, we don't have to trick our Father into blessing us. He is always eager to give blessings to His children. Aren't you thankful that God is always in a blessing mood? I hope you'll take time today to reflect on the ways God's blessings have changed your life, and that you'll begin to think of ways you can pass on those blessings.

Pray About It

God, Your blessings are far more than I deserve. Thank You for Your unconditional love and for the ways I see blessing overflowing in my own life. Make me like You in my ability and desire to bless others. Reveal to me those who need to hear a word of blessing, and give me the words and the courage to offer those words today. Amen.

Act On It

- Write a blessing for someone you love. Try to include some of the following elements: the power of positive words, the gift of unconditional love, some dreams or prayers you have for an outstanding future. When you are finished, send it in writing or read it verbally to the one you long to bless.

Day 5: Jacob the Prodigal

Read God's Word

[1] Jacob looked up and there was Esau, coming with his four hundred men; so he divided the children among Leah, Rachel and the two female servants. [2] He put the female servants and their children in front, Leah and her children next, and Rachel and Joseph in the rear. [3] He himself went on ahead and bowed down to the ground seven times as he approached his brother.

⁴ But Esau ran to meet Jacob and embraced him; he threw his arms around his neck and kissed him. And they wept. ⁵ Then Esau looked up and saw the women and children. "Who are these with you?" he asked.

Jacob answered, "They are the children God has graciously given your servant."

⁶ Then the female servants and their children approached and bowed down. ⁷ Next, Leah and her children came and bowed down. Last of all came Joseph and Rachel, and they too bowed down.

⁸ Esau asked, "What's the meaning of all these flocks and herds I met?"

"To find favor in your eyes, my lord," he said.

⁹ But Esau said, "I already have plenty, my brother. Keep what you have for yourself."

¹⁰ "No, please!" said Jacob. "If I have found favor in your eyes, accept this gift from me. For to see your face is like seeing the face of God, now that you have received me favorably. ¹¹ Please accept the present that was brought to you, for God has been gracious to me and I have all I need." And because Jacob insisted, Esau accepted it.

Genesis 33:1-11

Reflect and Respond

In my grandparents' sitting room were several large photo albums containing yellowed black-and-white pictures. Those albums also contained something more intangible: stories. If I sat with my grandmother with the albums open on her lap, she would turn the pages and tell me stories about these strangers who were actually relatives I had never met.

The stories those albums contained were from another era, but they always felt familiar—like the story about my grandfather's brother feeding a pig so much buttermilk that it was found belly-up the next morning; or the story of how my grandfather asked for my grandmother's hand in marriage by sitting awkwardly with her family all afternoon, with everyone knowing exactly why he was there, until he finally blurted out, "Well, I'm taking your daughter."

After years of hearing those stories, I could repeat them as though I had been there in person, when in reality most of them happened long before I was born.

In the same way, God's people have long held onto their heritage through the stories found in Scripture. By telling and retelling them, we have found an identity that started long before our stories on earth began.

Jesus had a way of rewriting the script of those old stories to give those who were listening new insight into both their own identity and God's character. Jesus once told a story that seemed very familiar to those who heard it because it sounded so much like the story of the reconciliation between Jacob and Esau.[5] While the story of Jacob and Esau is a true story about historical persons and Jesus' parable uses fictional characters to make a point, a comparison of the two stories has some interesting lessons to teach us.

Let's look together at the similarities and differences between the story that Jesus told and the closing of Jacob and Esau's fraternal conflict. We'll consider how they are alike, how they are different, and what Jesus was doing by changing the original story for new hearers. We may discover what Jesus wants us, the hearers of both stories, to apply to our own lives.

The last time we saw Jacob, he was at the bedside of his dying father, taking the last part of an inheritance that was not his, the blessing. Because of Esau's rage, Jacob has to immediately flee to a distant land to stay with relatives.

What is Esau's state of mind in Genesis 27:41?

He hated Jacob and wanted to kill him.

It's no wonder that, years later, Jacob is hesitant to burst in the door of his childhood home and announce his return. There is no way of knowing the extent of Esau's anger or how he might take revenge.

The story was well known to Jewish believers, who would have shaken their heads at Jacob's deviousness each time they heard it. Although they knew Jacob had questionable beginnings, they also identified him as a patriarch of their faith.

Read Genesis 32:28. What name is Jacob given during his return home? What does it mean?

Israel - for you have striven w/ God and w/ humans & have prevailed.

Jacob's new name came to describe the entire family: the nation of Israel. They took great pride in the stories that marked their spiritual pedigree.

Once Jesus was in conversation with a group of Jewish leaders who were criticizing Him.

What is their complaint in Luke 15:1-2?

That he was associating with sinful people - even eating w/ them

Instead of responding to their argument with an argument, Jesus started telling stories. Jesus was a master storyteller and held the crowd spellbound with a captivating story about a father and two sons. The story begins with a family drama over inheritance.

> *"You shall no longer be called Jacob, but Israel, for you have striven with God and with humans and have prevailed."*
> Genesis 32:28
> NRSV

135

Read Luke 15:11-32 to familiarize yourself with the story. (Use your pen or a bookmark to mark your place at Luke 15, and then turn to Genesis 33. You'll be referring to both texts as we continue together.)

What themes of Jacob and Esau's story do you recognize in this parable?

brothers fighting for father's approval

Those who listened to Jesus tell this story would have immediately recognized some of the echoes of Jacob and Esau's story. Both focus on family betrayal and the resulting conflict between two sons. In both, the younger son shocks the family by prizing his inheritance over his family and then running away to a far country.

There is also a notable difference between the two stories. Jacob's ultimate betrayal, the theft of his brother's birthright, occurred at his father's supposed deathbed—although Isaac ended up living longer (Genesis 35:28-29). Such an act of deception was a low-down, dirty trick to play on an elderly father who was sick and blind. But in Jesus' story, the younger son demands his part of the inheritance while his father is still alive and healthy. To the hearers of the story, this was a shocking plot twist. Kenneth Bailey, a scholar who lived for years in the Middle East and gained perspective from the ancient culture there, explains, "Such a request in village society means only one thing: *The younger son is impatient for his father's death.*"[6]

Basically, the younger son is saying that he wishes his father were dead and that all his family is good for is to give him the money he desires. He then leaves home for a "far country" to spend it all on shameful pursuits.

In both Jacob's true life story and the story Jesus told about the prodigal, the younger sons:

- receive their inheritance through dishonorable means,
- run away and seek happiness elsewhere,
- forfeit their ill-gotten inheritance—Jacob because he is not home to enjoy what is now his, and the prodigal because it has all been spent,
- care for livestock while they are away from home (Jacob's care of his uncle Laban's goats leads to a new collection of assets—livestock of his own—while the prodigal's occupation of caring for pigs, which were considered unclean by the Jews, is a true sign of his desperation), and
- reach a breaking point and decide to return home.

Despite their apprehension in returning home, both younger sons are welcomed with open arms. However, it's here that the stories diverge, because the welcoming character in the prodigal story is the father while the welcoming character in Jacob's story is his brother, Esau.

During his journey home, Jacob learns that his brother, Esau, is coming on the road to meet him accompanied by four hundred men. This sounds more like a war party than a welcoming party. Now, for the first time, instead of grasping other people's gifts, Jacob becomes a giver and sends gifts ahead to Esau as a peace offering.

The prodigal son travels home empty-handed with his tail tucked between his legs. Like Jacob, he wonders what kind of reception he will receive at home. Before he even reaches the house, however, his father sees him from a long way off and runs to meet him. The prodigal has prepared a speech asking to be given a position as a servant, but the father will hear nothing of it. He welcomes his younger son unconditionally and lavishes him with gifts to celebrate his return, once again marking him as a son and an heir.

Jacob sends gifts ahead to earn Esau's forgiveness. The prodigal has no gifts to give but receives gifts from his father when he arrives. Which do you think mirrors our returning to God and His reception of us?

he prodigal

Read Ephesians 2:8-9. From which perspective do these verses describe God?

As a loving God, expecting nothing but faith in Him.

Although Jacob approaches with gifts and the prodigal has none, in both of their stories we see that welcome is not based on worthiness. In fact, one of the most beautiful parallels between the two stories is the reception the two young men receive from their relative.

Reread Genesis 33:4. What does Esau do when he sees his brother?

(He runs to him, hugs & kisses him) & cries.

Read Luke 15:20. What does the father do when he sees his son?

He ran, hugged, & kissed him.

These are the only two places in Scripture where we find this exact description of running toward someone, throwing arms around him, and kissing him. The similarity between the stories, while implicit until now, becomes undeniably strong at this point. Those listening to Jesus' story would have noticed a very clear connection and leaned in closer to hear how Jesus would resolve the story.

For by grace you have been saved through faith, and this is not your own doing; it is the gift of God—not the result of works, so that no one may boast.
Ephesians 2:8-9
NRSV

The father in the prodigal story is clearly meant to mirror our heavenly Father, who eagerly awaits our return when we stray from Him and accepts us just as we are.

Reread Genesis 33:10. When Esau forgives Jacob, to what does Jacob compare seeing his brother's face?

like seeing the face of God

> God reveals Himself in the faces of those who offer forgiveness. When we are called to forgive others, our actions can reflect God's face and God's love.

God reveals Himself in the faces of those who offer forgiveness. When we are called to forgive others, our actions can reflect God's face and God's love. If we exhibit resentment and bitterness toward those who have wronged us or toward our heavenly Father, we are more like the older brother in the prodigal story who returned home angry that his brother had received what he did not deserve, and who was unwilling to offer forgiveness and grace.

As Jesus' story ended, his listeners may have realized that they were being cast in an unflattering role. While historically they had identified themselves with Jacob, the one called Israel who became the father of a great people, in Jesus' story they were the older brother, resentful that Jesus would welcome those who had lived lives of disobedience.

In the prodigal story, do you identify more with the son who has run away and returned home or with the son who has faithfully served?

The father figures in these two stories are very different. Jacob's father, Isaac, has always been aloof and detached. Easily fooled, he gives away the blessing to the wrong son; then when Esau asks for a different blessing, he proclaims a shortage of blessing: there is not enough to go around.

The prodigal's father, in contrast, cannot be manipulated or bought by his son's bargaining tactics. Instead, he gives away his wealth freely when asked, and he gives his blessing upon his son's return.

A final comparison has to do with a statement in each story that indicates an attitude toward blessing. In Jacob's story, when he is returning home, his uncle Laban surveys the livestock Jacob is taking with him and declares: "All you see is mine" (Genesis 31:43). The attitude expressed here is one of lack or insufficiency. Yet in Jesus' story, when the older son confronts his father about why the younger, misbehaving son is receiving special treatment, the father proclaims: "Everything I have is yours!" (Luke 15:31). The father reminds the older brother that there is more than enough blessing for both of his sons, more than enough to satisfy all of their needs.

These two stories help identify two roles we often find in our own family stories: the one who breaks away from the family and is in need of someone to welcome her or him back home, and the one who remains faithfully at home and serves but holds resentment toward others in the family who are not serving.

While Jacob and Esau's story is resolved with the reconciliation between the brothers, Jesus' parable is open-ended, allowing His listeners to finish the story. He seems to ask His listeners, *What will you do? How will you respond to the grace offered so freely not only to you but to anyone who wants to run into the open and waiting arms of the Father?*

How about you? How will you respond when God declares, "All that is mine is yours"? There is plenty to go around. Plenty for all. Plenty of love, plenty of forgiveness, plenty of grace.

Pray About It

Lord, Your offer of grace sometimes seems too good to be true. When I squander Your gifts, when I run away, when I find myself ashamed, You welcome me back. You run to meet me. Your face shines with love and acceptance. Help me to celebrate the grace You so freely offer not only to me but also to others. Let me be Your arms to welcome them home. Amen.

Act On It

- Are there families, perhaps even your own, that you know are in need of reconciliation? Pray for the return and reunion of family members separated by distance, whether emotional or physical.

- Are there family members, possibly even yours, who struggle with resentment because of the actions of others in the family? Pray for the softening of hearts, for forgiveness, and for faces that shine with the love of Christ.

Week 4
Video Viewer Guide

The oldest son inherited:

1. The Birthright— *physical* inheritance; right to place of authority in the family

2. The Blessing—confirmation that the oldest was the heir and new head of the family; *spiritual* inheritance of God's favor and blessings

Esau despised his birthright. (Genesis 25:34)

You were born with a kind of birthright—

the _details_ that make you _uniquely_ who you are.

Wishing you were someone you are not says you don't trust that God did a _good_ job with _you_ .

Blessing is part of God's job description. (Genesis 1:27-28)

Esau said to his father, "Do you have only _one_ *blessing, my father? Bless me* _too_ *, my father!" Then Esau wept aloud.*

Genesis 27:38 NIV

God always has more than enough ___blessing___ to go around.

If we're busy comparing our blessings to those of others, we won't see the blessings God is ___pouring___ out on us.

God _____ to bless you!

Week 5
Rachel and Leah

Anne obviously doesn't remember the day she was born, but she tells the story as if she is recounting it from memory. She was the fourth daughter born into a struggling family. Expenses were tight, and another mouth to feed wasn't purely joyous news for her parents. To make matters worse, her mother really wanted this fourth child to be a boy. When the doctors announced, "It's a girl!" she turned her face away, declining to even look at her newborn daughter.

Later that day Anne's grandfather sat beside his daughter's hospital bed, cradling the new baby in his arms. "What are you going to name her?" he asked. "Don't care," came the answer from the bed. He suggested, "How about Ann?" There was no response from Anne's mother at first, but eventually she answered: "If you're going to give her such a plain name, at least put an *e* on the end."

Anne's mother did not warm up to the new baby. In fact, her desire to interact with her youngest daughter did not extend much beyond feeding and changing her. Anne says she realizes now that postpartum depression probably played a role in her mother's lack of desire to bond with her as a child. As she grew older, Anne felt the sting of her mother's rejection again and again. She tried hard to please her mother by being quiet and well-behaved, but the more she acted like a good girl to win her mother's attention, the more invisible it seemed she became.

As a young woman, Anne's life was filled with the turmoil of one relationship after another as she sought the affirmation and affection she had never received as a child. Each relationship left her more scarred than the last. She had little contact with her family until one day her oldest sister asked if they could get together for lunch. Anne was a little suspicious. The four sisters had always seen each other as rivals, competing for the little bit of attention and love in a family when there seemed to be not enough to go around. Her oldest sister, Beth, had been grown and out of the house by the time Anne was in middle school, but when Anne agreed to meet with her she found Beth looked and acted like a different person than she remembered. Beth showed Anne warmth and acceptance, things she wasn't used to receiving from a family member. Her once-competitive

142

nature had turned affirming and friendly, and she seemed genuinely interested in Anne's life and hopeful for Anne's future.

While she was skeptical at first, Anne's damaged heart began to heal because of her newfound relationship with her sister. Beth became a strong maternal figure for her, helping to guide her in ways she had always longed for her own mother to do. One day Anne broke down and asked her sister, after all they had been through as children, how she could find the strength to love. Beth responded that she had been invited on a retreat by some friends from work, and it was there that she met Jesus Christ. His love had changed her and given her the desire to offer that same love to her own family. Anne eventually became a follower of Christ herself. Years later she and Beth were even able to pray over their mother together at her deathbed.

Family should be a warm and nurturing place where we begin to grow not only physically but also in confidence and trust. Unfortunately, not all families are equipped as such wonderful starting places to launch us into the world. This week we will see that Rachel and Leah not only grew up in the same flawed family as sisters, they even married the same man and created a large dysfunctional brood of their own! I hope that the insights we catch from the story of these sisters and their struggle for love will propel us in a direction opposite from theirs, encouraging us to choose to give rather than take, to love rather than despise, and to see family members as close allies and team members rather than competitors.

Day 1: Meet Me at the Well

Read God's Word

¹ Then Jacob continued on his journey and came to the land of the eastern peoples. ² There he saw a well in the open country, with three flocks of sheep lying near it because the flocks were watered from that well. The stone over the mouth of the well was large. ³ When all the flocks were gathered there, the shepherds would roll the stone away from the well's mouth and water the sheep. Then they would return the stone to its place over the mouth of the well.

⁴ Jacob asked the shepherds, "My brothers, where are you from?"

"We're from Harran," they replied.

⁵ He said to them, "Do you know Laban, Nahor's grandson?"

"Yes, we know him," they answered.

⁶ Then Jacob asked them, "Is he well?"

"Yes, he is," they said, "and here comes his daughter Rachel with the sheep."

⁷ "Look," he said, "the sun is still high; it is not time for the flocks to be gathered. Water the sheep and take them back to pasture."

⁸ "We can't," they replied, "until all the flocks are gathered and the stone has been rolled away from the mouth of the well. Then we will water the sheep."

⁹ While he was still talking with them, Rachel came with her father's sheep, for she was a shepherd. ¹⁰ When Jacob saw Rachel daughter of his uncle Laban, and Laban's sheep, he went over and rolled the stone away from the mouth of the well and watered his uncle's sheep. ¹¹ Then Jacob kissed Rachel and began to weep aloud. ¹² He had told Rachel that he was a relative of her father and a son of Rebekah. So she ran and told her father.

¹³ As soon as Laban heard the news about Jacob, his sister's son, he hurried to meet him. He embraced him and kissed him and brought him to his home, and there Jacob told him all these things. ¹⁴ Then Laban said to him, "You are my own flesh and blood."

Genesis 29:1-14

Reflect and Respond

Today we jump back into the middle of Jacob's journey to fill in the rest of the story of this generation. Those hearing the story of Jacob and Esau may think that no sibling story can match the struggles of this pair of brothers. This week we'll be introduced to a set of sisters that rival their status of "worst siblings ever."

Having swindled his brother's birthright and stolen his blessing, Jacob leaves town as quickly as possible. He sets off on the road to Harran, a pathway well-worn by his family. As we've seen, Abraham was the first in the family to travel that path from Harran to Canaan (Genesis 12:4-5) when God called him to leave his homeland for a promised land rich in provision, people, and the presence of God. Although this new land was their new home, they continued to make pilgrimages back home to visit the family left there and, more specifically, to find spouses for their sons.

Although our culture deems the marriage of close relatives taboo, in their culture a match made between cousins was considered a favorable one. Their closest ties were between family members within a clan or tribe. Why marry the girl next door if you don't even have to look outside the family compound?

We've also seen that years later Abraham's servant traveled the same route back to the family's homestead in Harran to find a wife for Isaac since Abraham was too old to make the journey. Through God's divine matchmaking the servant discovered Rebekah, and with the blessing of her brother, Laban, brought her back from Harran to Canaan.

Now Jacob sets off to trace these steps again back to the homeland of Harran. This is not a short journey. Five hundred miles of walking through hot desert-land is not a trip that anyone would make on a whim.

Read Genesis 28:1-5.

Who instructs Jacob to go on this journey? *Isaac*

How specific are his instructions about the identity of Jacob's future wife? *Don't marry any Canaanite women. Go to Paddan-aram, to the house of your grandfather, Bethuel, & marry one of your uncle Laban's daughters*

Read Genesis 27:42-44. What is the clandestine reason for sending Jacob back home?
Rebekah heard that Esau was planning to kill him. Stay w/ uncle until brother cools off.

Jacob arrives at his destination and finds himself at a well. It may not be the exact well where his grandfather's servant found a wife for his father, but once again a well proves itself a hotspot for meeting a woman.

The second meeting of a wife by a well in this family might seem especially coincidental (or providential) to us, but in those days a village well was a popular public gathering place, especially for women who performed many of the household duties for the family. Jacob's encounter with his future bride at what was literally a "local watering hole" may have been commonplace in those days. It would have been the equivalent of a common "meeting place" in our day, such as work, school, a connection through a friend, an online dating service, a bar or club, or a place of worship.[1]

Though it may seem strange to us that many of the Bible's love stories began through arranged marriage and even encounters at a well, do you think any of our culture's courting habits might have seemed alien to Jacob and his contemporaries? If so, which ones?

[A well] would have been the equivalent of a common "meeting place" in our day.

Jacob has just finished asking some local shepherds about his mother's brother, Laban, when an attractive shepherdess and her flock approach. As if on cue, the shepherds quip: "As a matter of fact, here comes Laban's daughter now!" Perhaps Jacob remembers stories of his grandfather's servant selecting his mother as a bride at a well in the same area. Jacob is taken with Rachel the moment he sees her. Ever the crafty one, he immediately tries to get rid of the shepherds for a moment alone with the approaching lovely shepherdess.[2]

How does Jacob try to divert the shepherds in Genesis 29:7?

Telling them to water the sheep & take them back to the pasture

Jacob finds out they are waiting for all the flocks to gather and for someone to roll the stone away from the front of the well so they can all water their sheep. When Rachel approaches, Jacob immediately takes action.

Take a look at Genesis 29:10. What two things does Jacob do?

rolled the stone away & water his uncle's sheep

First Jacob flexes his muscles and shows off his strength by rolling the stone in front of the well away. Then he waters his uncle's sheep as an act of service toward Rachel.

As negative as our stories of Jacob's character have been, it's heartwarming to see him do something out of kindness for someone else. Here, he is picking up a positive characteristic of his mother's instead of following her deceitful lead. After all, it was Jacob and Esau's mother, Rebekah, who watered the camels of Abraham's servant at a well before she ever knew that act would change her life forever. In this story the roles change as a man provides water for the flock of a young woman.

Jacob then weeps for joy with honest emotion and kisses Rachel as he shares the news that he is a close relative visiting from a far off land. Just as the man who brokered the marriage deal between Jacob's parents—Isaac and Rebekah—was taken directly from the well to meet Rebekah's brother, Laban, so Rachel immediately takes Jacob to meet her father, who just so happens to be Laban.

These two stories of back-to-back generations where meetings at a well provided a marriage and a future for a nation were well-known and loved by God's people. I wonder if young women who later heard these stories lingered just a little after their chores at the well, wondering if they might encounter a handsome young traveler or the servant of a rich man out looking for an eligible maiden. I also wonder what might have been going through the mind of a woman, centuries later, who encountered a man at a well in the same country, especially since the well she visited was clearly recorded as "Jacob's well."

We read about this woman in John 4. This woman who visits Jacob's well all these years later is there without camels or sheep, simply drawing water for her daily needs. The well she approaches is not the one where Jacob met Rebekah. Since it is in the area known as Samaria at this time, the well may be where Jacob bought land in Genesis 33:18-19.

This woman is there at the wrong time of day, since Scripture tells us that it is noon. Women normally would come to the well in the early morning or later in the day to avoid the heat, gathering there at a common time for both practicality and community. This particular woman may be there midday to avoid the other women, having been ostracized and gossiped about for her past choices and her tendency to try to fill the emptiness she feels inside by seeking the wrong kind of attention.

The man she meets at the well is not the servant of a rich man, but He does identify Himself as one who comes to serve. He won't display any vast acts of strength on this day, but later He will be credited with rolling away a stone that changes the course of history.

Turn to John 4 and answer the following questions:

Who is the man she encounters at the well? (v. 1)

Jesus

What does Jesus ask of her? (v. 7) *for a drink*

Why does she think this is an unusual request? (v. 9)

He was a Jew & she was a Samaritan woman

Why does Jesus say this is an unusual request? (v. 10)

"If only you knew the gift God has for you & who you are speaking to, you would ask me, & I would give you living water

147

In all of this back-and-forth discussion about Jesus providing a kind of water that is better than the water that comes from the well, the woman starts to question Jesus' claims. "Who do you think you are?" she seems to be saying. More specifically, she asks: "Are you greater than our father Jacob, who gave us this well?" (John 4:12). Here they are at Jacob's well, and this stranger seems to be promising that He can provide something greater than the ancestor she so reveres. (I've always thought it is interesting that Jacob, the scoundrel of the Genesis family, ends up with the reputation of a saint, being revered by his descendants.)

The beautiful promise of Jesus in John 4:13-14 seems to hit the spot for this woman who has been dry and thirsty for so long:

> *"Everyone who drinks this water will be thirsty again, but whoever drinks the water I give them will never thirst. Indeed, the water I give them will become in them a spring of water welling up to eternal life."*

It's not wrong to desire the love of other people. God wants us all to have lives rich in love relationships on many levels. But if we count on those relationships to satisfy our need for fulfillment, we will find ourselves dry and thirsty again and again.

When have you searched for happiness in something that did not satisfy?

How have you found satisfaction in Christ?

After the great legacy of these two Genesis stories about finding love at a well, the story of this woman provides us a new perspective on where to search for lifelong love. Here we have a story of a woman who seeks to fill the emptiness in her life in person after person. She has been looking for love in all the wrong places for quite some time now. Other women in her culture might daydream about finding lasting love at a well, in the tradition of Isaac and Rebekah and Jacob and Rachel. Instead, she finds lasting love of another kind.

The metaphor for the water that Jesus offers—living water—imagines love as a renewable resource, spilling out from within. When she finally realizes the potential of this new, overflowing love Jesus offers, the woman does something significant.

What does John 4:28-29 tell us that she does?

Ran back to village to tell everyone she said to come see the man who might be the Messiah

God wants us all to have lives rich in love relationships on many levels. But if we count on those relationships to satisfy our need for fulfillment, we will find ourselves dry and thirsty again and again.

I love that Scripture tells us that she drops her water jar and runs back to town. In a way, it lets us know that she is giving up finding sustenance in worldly ways, leaving behind the broken jars of relationships that have left her empty and seeking. Unlike the temporary fix of the love she has sought in the past, the water Jesus offers is overflowing with new life.

We all have the desire to find the satisfaction of true love. For Jacob and Rachel, it began at a well. For this woman, her encounter led her to love of an eternal kind, love that never fails. Where are you looking for love? Find it in Jesus, and you will find it becomes a spring of life within you, filling you up and spilling out onto others.

Pray About It

Lord, help me seek to have my deepest needs met in You. Where I've searched for satisfaction in other places, heal the cracks and brokenness that have formed. Fill me up with Your love so that I may spill Your love onto others. Amen.

Act On It

- Read Jeremiah 2:13. Ask God to reveal the "broken cisterns" in your own life. Invite Jesus right now to fill you to overflowing with his everlasting love.

Day 2: Here Comes the Bride(s)

Read God's Word

¹³ As soon as Laban heard the news about Jacob, his sister's son, he hurried to meet him. He embraced him and kissed him and brought him to his home, and there Jacob told him all these things. ¹⁴ Then Laban said to him, "You are my own flesh and blood."

¹⁵ After Jacob had stayed with him for a whole month, Laban said to him, "Just because you are a relative of mine, should you work for me for nothing? Tell me what your wages should be."

¹⁶ Now Laban had two daughters; the name of the older was Leah, and the name of the younger was Rachel. ¹⁷ Leah had weak eyes, but Rachel had a lovely figure and was beautiful. [18] *Jacob was in love with Rachel and said, "I'll work for you seven years in return for your younger daughter Rachel."*

[19] *Laban said, "It's better that I give her to you than to some other man. Stay here with me."* [20] *So Jacob served seven years to get Rachel, but they seemed like only a few days to him because of his love for her.*

[21] *Then Jacob said to Laban, "Give me my wife. My time is completed, and I want to make love to her."*

[22] *So Laban brought together all the people of the place and gave a feast.* [23] *But when evening came, he took his daughter Leah and brought her to Jacob, and Jacob made love to her.* [24] *And Laban gave his servant Zilpah to his daughter as her attendant.*

[25] *When morning came, there was Leah! So Jacob said to Laban, "What is this you have done to me? I served you for Rachel, didn't I? Why have you deceived me?"*

[26] *Laban replied, "It is not our custom here to give the younger daughter in marriage before the older one.* [27] *Finish this daughter's bridal week; then we will give you the younger one also, in return for another seven years of work."*

[28] *And Jacob did so. He finished the week with Leah, and then Laban gave him his daughter Rachel to be his wife.* [29] *Laban gave his servant Bilhah to his daughter Rachel as her attendant.* [30] *Jacob made love to Rachel also, and his love for Rachel was greater than his love for Leah. And he worked for Laban another seven years.*

Genesis 29:13-30

Reflect and Respond

Jacob was smitten with Rachel from the moment he saw her herding sheep toward the well. He was given explicit instructions from his father to marry one of Laban's daughters, so I'm sure he was delighted when he discovered that's exactly who this beautiful young woman was. What he didn't know yet was that Laban had two daughters, and that simple fact set off enough drama to fill his life for many years.

Reread Genesis 29:16-17.

What do you learn about Rachel from this passage?

had a lovely figure & was beautiful

What do you learn about Leah?

weak eyes

I don't know about you, but when I read this passage it stirs up my sympathy for Leah immediately.

Rachel is described as having a lovely figure and as beautiful. Basically she has a stunning face and a great body. And Leah—the only description we hear about her involves her eyes. The Hebrew word used to describe Leah's eyes, *rakkot*, is often translated "weak," possibly referring to her eyesight or a medical problem with her eyes.[3] The best-case scenario (for Leah anyway) is that it may be a compliment, since the phrase also can be translated "delicate eyes." Leah may have tender eyes, but Jacob has eyes only for Rachel.

The passage raves about Rachel, but when it comes to Leah, all it says is she has nice eyes. This might be the equivalent of us saying that one sister was gorgeous and the other had a "nice personality." To add insult to insult, Rachel's name means "ewe lamb," a tender picture of a young female sheep—and perhaps a nod to her occupation as shepherdess—while the name Leah means either "weary" or "cow."[4]

Can't you see the strain of comparison between these two sisters already? I'm sure they grew up hearing people compare their looks and their names. Even the Bible begins their story by casting them as rivals. How can they not spend their lives comparing themselves to each other?

The problems for Jacob begin when he and Laban strike up a deal. Jacob will work for Laban for seven years as payment for marrying the daughter who is lovely. There is no handshake on this deal, no covenant made, no celebratory meal described. Jacob takes Laban at his word, a mistake he will later regret. Even the crafty Jacob can be blinded by love, and he lets his guard down.

What does Laban tell Jacob in Genesis 29:14?

You are my own flesh & blood

Laban's declaration is true in more ways than one. Their similarities are lost on Jacob at first, but later he may come to recognize the family traits of manipulation that have been passed down from Eve to Sarah to his mother, Rebekah, and her brother, Laban.

The clues to Laban's character are there from the beginning. Beginning in verse 10, when Jacob first realizes his family connection to Rachel, the text refers not once but three times to Laban as Jacob's uncle, literally in the original language "the brother of my mother."[5] The repeated references to Rebekah encourage us to remember her manipulative antics in orchestrating the plan for her younger son to take the blessing of the elder. Since Rebekah and Laban were raised in the same household and formed by the same family "script," it's no wonder they learned games of deception, possibly beginning with the antics passed between them when they were growing up together.

Rachel means "ewe lamb."

Leah means "weary" or "cow."

Laban reveals his true colors soon enough. Although Jacob's understanding is that he is toiling for seven years to win the hand of Rachel, who is beautiful, Laban has other plans. So when the seven years are complete and the wedding arrives, Laban sets his plan into motion and throws a feast in honor of his daughter's wedding.

Reread Genesis 29:22-25. What does Laban do next?

Brought Together people for a feast.
He took Leah to Jacob & he made love to her, thinking it was Rachel.

Jacob, possibly having feasted a little more than his limit, stumbles into a dark tent with a veiled bride and doesn't realize until the morning that he has been duped. He has been given the wrong sister. He thinks he is going to bed with the beautiful lamb but awakes with the cow.

The plot of this story unfolds masterfully with suspense and humor. As the onlookers, we know that Jacob has been tricked, and we are waiting for the other shoe to drop and the realization to hit him. His confrontation of Laban is a strangely satisfying episode because we recognize that Jacob has been wronged and, at the same time, is getting what he has coming.

Genesis 29:25 provides a dramatic culmination of the scheme.

What does Jacob say to Laban in verse 25?

What have you done to me? I served you for 7 yrs for Rachel.

What excuse does Laban give in verse 26?

The youngest doesn't get married before the oldest

In perfect symmetry Jacob, the younger brother who has swindled his older brother out of his entitlements (with the help of his father's darkened eyes), becomes the victim (in the dark nonetheless) of a plot where the older daughter seizes what was supposed to belong to the younger.

Don't miss the ironic confrontation when Jacob declares that Laban has "deceived" him. Because Jacob's name literally means Deceiver, he is actually shouting, "Why have you '*Jacobed*' me?" In a moment of clear comeuppance, someone has out-Jacobed the Jacob. It turns out Uncle Laban uses "the old switcheroo" that Jacob practiced on his brother, and now the older to younger thievery has been reversed.

I wonder if Jacob realizes the irony of what he is saying the moment the words come out of his mouth. He is condemning the very act he has perpetrated in his own family. In fact, when Laban insists that this is Leah's right because she is the "firstborn"—using the same Hebrew word, *bekor*, used in previous chapters for Esau's position—Jacob does not object.[6] (Though you would think someone would have mentioned this "right" during the preceding seven years of hard work!)

While I would like to sit back and shake my head at Jacob's antics and then revel when he gets his just reward, I have to admit that the way he is suddenly confronted with his own flaws has occurred in my own life more times than I'd like to admit. I meet someone who somehow rubs me the wrong way, and when I finally put my finger on what this person does that bugs me, I realize that it's one of my flaws too! God uses someone else to show me what I should be paying attention to in my own life. When we have a flaw in our character that we're unaware of, God sometimes holds up a mirror to us in the form of another person to show us just what it is that needs to change.

Can you think of something that irritates you in other people that is actually a flaw of your own?

Read Luke 6:42. What was Jesus' advice to us when we notice flaws in others?

Look at your own flaws before you criticize others

Jacob is seeing his own flaws reflected in his Uncle Laban, and he's experiencing firsthand the kind of pain and disappointment that he caused to his own brother. And just as Jacob offered no apology to Esau, Laban offers no apology to Jacob. Instead he offers another deal.

What solution does Laban present in Genesis 29:27?

Work 7 more yrs. for Rachel

If something like this were to happen in our time, the situation probably would produce a quick annulment or divorce. In their culture, the answer was marrying the second sister as well, since polygamy was a common practice.

The plot in this story so far has centered around the men—Laban's deception and Jacob's shock. But what about the women behind the scenes? We don't know when Rachel and Leah are brought up to speed on their father's plot to deceive their future husband, but they at least have to go along with it by the wedding night.

As we watch the story unfold, remember that Rachel and Leah are living in a time when women are relegated to background roles in a rather mundane

"Or how can you say to your neighbor, 'Friend, let me take out the speck in your eye,' when you yourself do not see the log in your own eye? You hypocrite, first take the log out of your own eye, and then you will see clearly to take the speck out of your neighbor's eye."
Luke 6:42 NRSV

153

existence. Their wedding feast is one of the few times they are given honor and attention. Both women probably have been looking forward to their weddings since they were little girls, knowing that the elaborate celebration will last up to two weeks with all their family and friends in attendance and them at the center.

Just think how Rachel must feel when, after the first week of her wedding feast, her father chooses to give her husband to her sister instead. And consider how Leah must feel being robbed of her own moment in the spotlight. She even has to endure the look of horror on her husband's face at the realization that he has married her. Even though a deal is struck that means they will finish the second half of the feast for what is Leah's wedding celebration and continue immediately into Rachel's wedding celebration, those must be parties that are more bitter than sweet for both young women. Instead of dancing at one another's weddings as bridesmaids, these two sisters are being set up for a future life together under the same roof married to the same man—one in which they will continue to compete for attention, affection, and love.

In this imperfect world, disappointment is an unfortunate fact of life. Like Rachel and Leah, some of us have been wronged deeply by those we trust. Like Jacob, at times our heartfelt hopes and expectations have not been met. And yet in another scene of deception and brokenness within this imperfect family, we see that God continues to walk beside them. God is not surprised, nor are His plans foiled, by Laban's tricks. He continues to sing over Rachel in her disappointment and to see beauty in Leah when she feels ignored. And in your own story, God continues to watch over you, too, no matter where you find yourself.

Pray About It

Dear Jesus, remind me today of the beauty You see in me. When I am disappointed or feel overlooked, whisper in my ear the message of Your deep and undying love. Give me Your eyes to see those who feel invisible in life so that I can pour out Your love on them. Amen.

Act On It

- **Have you ever resented someone else's moment in the spotlight, wishing it were you receiving the attention? Describe how you felt:**

- **Now read Luke 12:6-7 and Zephaniah 3:17. How does it feel to know God lavishes you with such intimate attention that you are always in His spotlight, with no detail beyond His notice?**

Undeserving blessed

- Give thanks for God's abundant love and blessings for you and for the person you named. Ask God to help you release your resentment toward this person and to celebrate God's goodness in both of your lives.

Day 3: Barrenness and Blessing

Read God's Word

¹ *When Rachel saw that she was not bearing Jacob any children, she became jealous of her sister. So she said to Jacob, "Give me children, or I'll die!"*
² *Jacob became angry with her and said, "Am I in the place of God, who has kept you from having children?"*

Genesis 30:1-2

¹ *There was a certain man from Ramathaim, a Zuphite from the hill country of Ephraim, whose name was Elkanah son of Jeroham, the son of Elihu, the son of Tohu, the son of Zuph, an Ephraimite.* ² *He had two wives; one was called Hannah and the other Peninnah. Peninnah had children, but Hannah had none....*
¹⁰ *In her deep anguish Hannah prayed to the LORD, weeping bitterly.* ¹¹ *And she made a vow, saying, "LORD Almighty, if you will only look on your servant's misery and remember me, and not forget your servant but give her a son, then I will give him to the Lord for all the days of his life, and no razor will ever be used on his head."*
¹² *As she kept on praying to the LORD, Eli observed her mouth.* ¹³ *Hannah was praying in her heart, and her lips were moving but her voice was not heard. Eli thought she was drunk* ¹⁴ *and said to her, "How long are you going to stay drunk? Put away your wine."*
¹⁵ *"Not so, my lord," Hannah replied, "I am a woman who is deeply troubled. I have not been drinking wine or beer; I was pouring out my soul to the LORD.* ¹⁶ *Do not take your servant for a wicked woman; I have been praying here out of my great anguish and grief."*

¹⁷ Eli answered, "Go in peace, and may the God of Israel grant you what you have asked of him."

¹⁸ She said, "May your servant find favor in your eyes." Then she went her way and ate something, and her face was no longer downcast.

¹⁹ Early the next morning they arose and worshiped before the LORD and then went back to their home at Ramah. Elkanah made love to his wife Hannah, and the LORD remembered her. ²⁰ So in the course of time Hannah became pregnant and gave birth to a son. She named him Samuel, saying, "Because I asked the LORD for him."

1 Samuel 1:1-2, 10-20

Reflect and Respond

Earlier in our study we explored God's promises to Abraham and Sarah. To illustrate the promise of blessings to come, God took Abraham outside and gave him a heavenly view of the future: "'Look up at the sky and count the stars—if indeed you can count them.' Then he said to him, 'So shall your offspring be'" (Genesis 15:5).

Do you recall what happened next? Was it an instant houseful of children, leading quickly to grandchildren and great-grandchildren? Did God's fulfilled promises fall into their lap like manna from heaven? You know that, unfortunately, the answer is no. The family of God, which He promised would become as fruitful as the stars, immediately began a struggle of barrenness.

Read the following Scriptures and identify which generations in Abraham's family struggled with the inability to have children.

Genesis 16:1 Sarai

Genesis 25:21 Rebekah

Genesis 30:1 Rachel

God's great promise of abundance to this family is instantly followed by three generations of great barriers to that promise. Three generations of childlessness in a row signals us to pay greater attention to a recurring theme in the Bible and to begin asking questions. What are we supposed to learn from the recurring theme of infertility in Scripture? I'd like us to explore four things we can learn today from the struggle of yesterday, beginning with the Genesis family and continuing in the stories of other biblical women.

1. God's faithfulness is bigger than our afflictions.

The road to the fulfillment of God's blessings is rarely an easy one. For those of us who hoped that committing our lives to Christ would bring only sunshine and smooth paths, Abraham's family story provides a stark but truthful reality: those who love God struggle too. But no matter how big the burdens in our lives may be, we know that God is bigger still. God designed our lives and our world to bring glory to Him no matter what circumstances we may face.

When, after long periods of agonizing waiting, God brings the miraculous blessing of a child to each of these three generations in Genesis, the answers to their prayers bring glory to God. This is especially true in Abraham and Sarah's story. Because of their advanced age, their son Isaac's birth is clearly a miracle to everyone who meets them. God loves to take on difficult stories in order to show His miraculous power, and bringing about the birth of a new nation through a family that has fought such an uphill battle to have children is a story that clearly shows God's power. Perhaps one of the reasons God chose Abraham's family was so that people would see His power on display in their lives.

Read these Scriptures about the power of our God, and write a few words next to each describing what you learn.

1 Chronicles 29:11 _Everything in the heavens and earth are His._

2 Chronicles 20:6 _Ruler of all the kingdoms of the earth. You are powerful + mighty_

Matthew 19:26 _with God everything is possible_

1 Corinthians 6:14 _God will raise us from the dead by His power_

Ephesians 3:20 _God, through His mighty power can accomplish infinitely more than we might ask or think._

Of course, God's love and power are also present in the lives of those who are never able to conceive children naturally (as well as those who choose not to

> The road to the fulfillment of God's blessings is rarely an easy one. . . . Those who love God struggle too. But no matter how big the burdens in our lives may be, we know that God is bigger still.

157

> Sometimes the answers to our prayers do not arrive as ordered. Yet there is one thing we can be sure of: God always answers our prayers with His presence and His blessings, even if we do not have eyes to see them at the time.

have children). But in light of my own struggle with infertility, I am especially sensitive to those who continue to struggle with childlessness. Not all couples who desire to have children see their prayers answered in the ways they have hoped. As we see in the Scriptures and experience in our own lives, sometimes the answers to our prayers do not arrive as ordered. Yet there is one thing we can be sure of: God always answers our prayers with His presence and His blessings, even if we do not have eyes to see them at the time.

2. The gift of life is a gift from God.

Living in the modern era of medicine, we understand far more about how each life begins than any generation before us. Yet even with our medical understanding of how cells join and multiply, those of us with faith still recognize that there is an element of childbearing that is a mystery, an act of creation outside of our control. As much as procreation is a scientific process, it is also filled with the concepts of hope, new life, and God and His blessings.

When people of faith face the overwhelming challenge of infertility, no matter what role medicine plays in helping to solve the problem, we know to turn to God for help. In fact, we may be more in touch with God's role as Creator when we pray for the hoped-for arrival of the smallest members of humankind. Families and communities praying for long-awaited babies remind us about God's mysterious role in creation.

Read Psalm 139:13-16. What do these verses say about the part God plays in our earliest days? *God was totally in control. We are formed through God*

Whether children are conceived naturally and quickly or after much struggle and waiting, we have a sense of awe that God is creating new life. This wonder-filled gratitude seems to be even more pronounced when children are born after extended periods of waiting and prayer. We need to hold onto the fact that children are a gift from God. (It also helps us to keep perspective when they act like anything but a blessing!) The stories of miraculous births in Scripture remind us to praise God for each and every life He has created.

Hannah's story, which opens the Book of First Samuel, is the most detailed story in the Bible of a woman crying out to God in her unfulfilled desire for children. From her we learn of painful periods of despair and depression (1:7), the strain on her marriage (1:8), and her continual expression of the deep desire of her heart to God.

How would you describe Hannah's prayers in 1 Samuel 1:12-16? *She was pouring her heart out to God. She was praying out of anguish and sorrow.*

When have you prayed for something that was a deep desire of your heart, and what was the outcome?

Because of her prolonged waiting and struggle, and because she knows God will answer her prayers, Hannah realizes from the beginning that Samuel belongs to God.

Read 1 Samuel 1:21-28.

What does Hannah do after Samuel is weaned?

She took him to the Tabernacle in Shiloh (to leave him w/ the Lord permanently) they brought a 3yr. old bull for the sacrifice & a basket of floor d wine. She presented him to Eli

Do you think this is difficult for her? Why or why not?

Of course, giving up your son would be hard, but she stuck to her promise.

Although not every child's story begins with such a dramatic episode, every child is a miracle of God. Although not every parent sends a child away to serve God for a lifetime, every parent can realize that his or her child belongs to God and has a special purpose in His kingdom. These stories from Scripture help us realize that every life is a gift to be treasured.

3. Those who struggle need our compassion and prayers.

Reading the stories of Sarah, Rebekah, and Rachel has always been a very personal exercise for me. When my husband, Jim, and I went through several painful years of infertility and multiple miscarriages, life felt like a constant roller coaster of hope and despair. Knowing God was with us was a comfort, of course, but sometimes we felt distant from God in our grief. It was the relationships with and support of other Christians that helped us to feel close to God again, even when our dreams were still far off.

Those who are facing this incredible battle often feel isolated and hopeless. Infertility can be difficult for the body and the emotions, but it can also produce strain on one's marriage, bank account, and faith.

Rather than well-meaning words of advice or success stories about others you have known, someone going through this difficult time may need your prayers, a listening ear, and an offer to be there when needed. Don't pull away from a friendship because you don't want to hurt someone by mentioning your own children or family. Give the relationship the same attention and warmth as always, with an offer to listen when needed. This same advice holds true for any friends who may be experiencing other kinds of struggles within their families.

What do you think is the best way you can help those who are wrestling with tough issues in their life and family? Write down two or three ideas.

Prayers
listen

If you know someone who has struggled with infertility, ask this person the best (and perhaps the worst) things people did to try to help.

4. These family stories of waiting help us understand the waiting family of God.

The Gospel of Luke opens not with the story of Jesus' arrival but the story of another pregnancy—the account of a childless couple named Zechariah and Elizabeth, an older relative of Mary's who suddenly finds herself pregnant.

Read Luke 1:39-41. When Mary and Elizabeth meet in this story, what happens? *Elizabeth's child leaped within her, & Elizabeth was filled w/the Holy Spirit.*

The juxtaposition of these two pregnant women—one young, unmarried, and expecting a baby that was totally unexpected, and the other an older childless woman who thought her years for expectancy were over—reminds us of something very significant about the people of God: their waiting.

Although Jesus came to an unwed teenage girl and her fiancé who were not expecting His arrival, the people of God had been waiting and crying out for the Messiah to come for many, many years. Elizabeth's appearance in the Christmas story reminds us that, not unlike an infertile couple, God's people had almost given up hope for Jesus' arrival.

God's people are a waiting people. We waited for the birth of Christ and for our redemption through His death and resurrection, and now we are waiting for His return and for the world to be returned to the original, intended state that God created in Eden.

Read Romans 8:19-22. What is waiting and groaning in this passage? *Waiting eagerly for that future day when God will reveal who his children really area. The creation looks forward to the day when it will join Gods children in glorious freedom from death & decay.*

We've all experienced times of waiting. At one time or another and in one way or another, we've all felt "barren," waiting on God's timing or plan to be revealed in our lives. The good news is that God uses our barrenness and times of waiting to prepare us for the blessings to come. Even now God is working and molding us into the image of His Son as we wait on His return and the restoration of all things. I pray that this hope-filled promise not only will sustain you in your own personal times of waiting but also will fill you with an unexplainable joy.

Pray About It

Almighty God, I praise You for Your greatness and majesty and power. Nothing is impossible for You! I am so thankful that Your faithfulness is greater than my afflictions—greater than any disappointment, delay, or detour I might ever face. Thank You for the hope we have in You. Use my times of waiting to prepare me for the blessings yet to come. Amen.

Act On It

- **What are the "barren" places in your life right now? Is there something you are waiting for God to do for you, in you, or through you? Ask God how He is using this time of barrenness and waiting to prepare you for what is to come. Write a prayer below, expressing your willingness to wait.**

- Think of someone you know who is struggling with a difficult issue or situation (perhaps infertility). Extend an expression of love and care and offer a listening ear to your friend today.

Day 4: Keeping Score

Read God's Word

29 [31] *When the LORD saw that Leah was not loved, he enabled her to conceive, but Rachel remained childless.* [32] *Leah became pregnant and gave birth to a son. She named him Reuben, for she said, "It is because the LORD has seen my misery. Surely my husband will love me now."*

> God uses our barrenness and times of waiting to prepare us for the blessings to come.

³³ *She conceived again, and when she gave birth to a son she said, "Because the L*ORD *heard that I am not loved, he gave me this one too." So she named him Simeon.*

³⁴ *Again she conceived, and when she gave birth to a son she said, "Now at last my husband will become attached to me, because I have borne him three sons." So he was named Levi.*

³⁵ *She conceived again, and when she gave birth to a son she said, "This time I will praise the L*ORD*." So she named him Judah. Then she stopped having children.*

30 ¹ *When Rachel saw that she was not bearing Jacob any children, she became jealous of her sister. So she said to Jacob, "Give me children, or I'll die!"*

² *Jacob became angry with her and said, "Am I in the place of God, who has kept you from having children?"*

³ *Then she said, "Here is Bilhah, my servant. Sleep with her so that she can bear children for me and I too can build a family through her."*

⁴ *So she gave him her servant Bilhah as a wife. Jacob slept with her,* ⁵ *and she became pregnant and bore him a son.* ⁶ *Then Rachel said, "God has vindicated me; he has listened to my plea and given me a son." Because of this she named him Dan.*

⁷ *Rachel's servant Bilhah conceived again and bore Jacob a second son.* ⁸ *Then Rachel said, "I have had a great struggle with my sister, and I have won." So she named him Naphtali.*

⁹ *When Leah saw that she had stopped having children, she took her servant Zilpah and gave her to Jacob as a wife.* ¹⁰ *Leah's servant Zilpah bore Jacob a son.* ¹¹ *Then Leah said, "What good fortune!" So she named him Gad.*

¹² *Leah's servant Zilpah bore Jacob a second son.* ¹³ *Then Leah said, "How happy I am! The women will call me happy." So she named him Asher.*

¹⁴ *During wheat harvest, Reuben went out into the fields and found some mandrake plants, which he brought to his mother Leah. Rachel said to Leah, "Please give me some of your son's mandrakes."*

¹⁵ *But she said to her, "Wasn't it enough that you took away my husband? Will you take my son's mandrakes too?"*

"Very well," Rachel said, "he can sleep with you tonight in return for your son's mandrakes."

¹⁶ *So when Jacob came in from the fields that evening, Leah went out to meet him. "You must sleep with me," she said. "I have hired you with my son's mandrakes." So he slept with her that night.*

¹⁷ *God listened to Leah, and she became pregnant and bore Jacob a fifth son.* ¹⁸ *Then Leah said, "God has rewarded me for giving my servant to my husband." So she named him Issachar.*

¹⁹ *Leah conceived again and bore Jacob a sixth son.* ²⁰ *Then Leah said, "God has presented me with a precious gift. This time my husband will treat me with honor, because I have borne him six sons." So she named him Zebulun.*

²¹ Some time later she gave birth to a daughter and named her Dinah.

²² Then God remembered Rachel; he listened to her and enabled her to conceive. ²³ She became pregnant and gave birth to a son and said, "God has taken away my disgrace." ²⁴ She named him Joseph, and said, "May the LORD add to me another son."

Genesis 29:31–30:24

Reflect and Respond

During a Christian leadership training workshop I attended, we were divided into teams and told that we were going to play a game. The object was to get as many points as possible before the exercise ended. As the rest of the rules were explained, you could look around the room and immediately spot those with more competitive natures, as their eyes began to glow with the unmistakable desire to win at all costs.

Each round of the game involved each team making one of three possible choices: option A meant that our team would get points, option B meant that other teams would get points, and option C meant that all teams would gain equal points. The only catch was that if every team chose option A, trying to gain points only for themselves, we all would lose points. Even though we knew that was a risk, round after round all the teams chose option A, and that meant we all ended with negative points. Despite the fact that this was a group of Christian leaders, promises were broken, lies told, and feelings hurt, all in the name of winning.

Finally, the facilitator revealed the secret of the exercise: the only way teams ever ended up with a positive number of points in the end was to consistently band together and choose to gain points for all teams slowly and equally. She surprised us by explaining that the goal, which was "to get as many points as possible," never meant that we had to compete against the other teams at all. Our competitive spirit had simply run away with us. Our desire to win by dominating others made us all losers in the end.

Discovering that competition hurts during a workshop exercise can be enlightening. Living that lesson every day in your family hurts on a far deeper level.

Rachel and Leah began their marriages to the same man within a week of each other. If anyone ever felt the sting of competition, these two sisters found themselves embroiled in a family drama that is hard for us to even imagine. Arranged marriage and polygamy are foreign concepts to us, but the idea that two sisters could be married to the same man at the same time is unthinkable. Anyone could guess that this arrangement is a disaster waiting to happen.

163

None of the relationships within this familial love triangle are prepped for success, especially because both sisters find themselves in a situation where they do not have the thing they long for most.

Later, a law is written in Leviticus about exactly this situation. What does Leviticus 18:18 say? *While your wife is living, do not marry her sister & have sexual relations w/ her, for they would be rivals.*

Leah is the underdog in the beginning because of her looks and the way her father deceived her husband into marrying her. It's very clear that Jacob is in love with Rachel but has to take Leah as part of the package.

Rachel may be the best-loved by their husband, but she's unable to have children, a fact that causes her great pain and distress. Leah has several sons right away, and Rachel is worried that her sister is pulling ahead of her in this competition. So Rachel comes up with this ingenious plan.

Reread Genesis 30:3. What is Rachel's plan? *She told Jacob to take her servant, Bilhah, sleep w/ her, so she can bear children for her*

Sound familiar? This is the exact same plan that caused Sarah so much trouble with Hagar and Ishmael. I wonder if Rachel realizes that this plan has already been used by Jacob's grandmother, and it didn't work out so well.

Leah, not to be outdone, pulls the same trick by having her maid Zilpah bear children with Jacob. Now we have four women in the same household sleeping with the same man.

Unfortunately for the children, Rachel and Leah use them to keep score in their rivalry. They're not the first family, nor are they the last, to use their children to compete, compare, and try to win status. This kind of ranking-by-children still goes on today.

I have small children, and I'm amazed at how many moms compare their toddlers and compete for earliest milestones in things such as learning the ABC's or writing their names. These moms are likely to find themselves comparing grades, awards, and athletic abilities as their children grow.

What are some ways you have seen parents comparing their children?
little

How do you think this affects children and families?

Leah and Rachel use their children's births to keep score. Here's a scoreboard of their children, indicating each child's place in the birth order.

Leah's children		Rachel's children	
Leah	Zilpah (Leah's servant)	Rachel	Bilhah (Rachel's servant)
1. Reuben	7. Gad	11. Joseph	5. Dan
2. Simeon	8. Asher	12. Benjamin	6. Naphtali
3. Levi			
4. Judah			
9. Issachar			
10. Zebulun			

Review today's Scripture from Genesis 29 and 30, and find the reasons these sisters give some of their children the names they do. Write a few of the boys' names and the reasons for their names here:

Reuben - because the Lord has seen my misery
Simeon - " " ; heard that she wasn't loved
Judah - to praise the Lord

In the end, Rachel bears Jacob two sons. Her story has a sad ending, though, because she dies giving birth to her younger son.

Read Genesis 35:16-18. What name does Rachel originally give her younger son (meaning "son of my trouble")? (v. 18)

Ben-oni

What does Jacob change it to (meaning "son of my right hand")? (v. 18)

Benjamin

I wonder how Leah mourned her sister's death. Did she grieve the years they lost by being in constant competition and rivalry with each other? Did she grieve the relationship they might have had, the support they might have given, the gift of watching each other's children grow up in the same house with love and support and affection? And then Leah was left alone to care for the whole brood, her children as well as her sister's. When family members compete, no one wins in the end.

How have you experienced or witnessed competition in your own family?

I recently met with a couple to talk about their upcoming wedding ceremony. They both had been married previously and shared with me that their preteen and teenage children were struggling with the idea of combining their two families into one. I've always considered it important to involve the children of the bride and groom in wedding ceremonies so that they feel a part of the newly formed family. I let the couple know of the many ways I've seen that done in the past: ceremonial gifts given from stepparents to their new stepchildren, flower arrangements created in which each family member adds a separate flower, and even families who pour different colors of sand into a single vase to create an heirloom they will keep in a prominent place in their new home to show that they value the masterpiece God is creating by combining their families together.

As we talked about the four kids and their various personalities, it became clear this was a very athletic family, since each of the children was involved and gifted in a different sport. We came up with a plan for the ceremony that we felt would be meaningful to the children and to those in attendance. When the time came in the wedding ceremony, I turned from the bride and groom and addressed their children using the metaphor of a team. Each player wears their own name, but the most important name on their jersey is the team name. In a team sport, when one team member struggles, the rest of the team finds ways to support and help; and when one scores, they all benefit. It takes the whole team pulling in the same direction to win. These children would grow up with different last names, but the important thing for them to keep in mind is that they are a team together. We then put our hands in the center of a circle, and they answered "we do" to a vow to support the new family and be part of a new team. At the reception, their parents gave them each a jersey with their names on the front and the family name written across the back. These parents loved their children and wanted to encourage them from the beginning to grow into one cohesive family.

Rachel and Leah remind us that God created families to operate as teams, not as competitors. When one family member hurts, we all hurt. When one family member succeeds, we all win. Instead of competing for some invisible rank in life, we do better to support our teammates with our words, our presence, and our affirmation.

Who is on your team? How can you support them today?

> God created families to operate as teams, not as competitors. When one family member hurts, we all hurt. When one family member succeeds, we all win.

Lord, I confess a spirit of competition often determines how I view others in my community and my family. Instead of believing that they must lose in order for me to win, help me to see us as one team and to support those closest to me with the love and grace You have lavished on me. Amen.

- **Make a list below (or on a separate sheet of paper) of those in your family—or the friends who form your family of choice. Next to these names, write ways that you can support and encourage them today.**

Day 5: Leaving Laban

Read God's Word

²² *On the third day Laban was told that Jacob had fled.* ²³ *Taking his relatives with him, he pursued Jacob for seven days and caught up with him in the hill country of Gilead.* ²⁴ *Then God came to Laban the Aramean in a dream at night and said to him, "Be careful not to say anything to Jacob, either good or bad."*

²⁵ *Jacob had pitched his tent in the hill country of Gilead when Laban overtook him, and Laban and his relatives camped there too.* ²⁶ *Then Laban said to Jacob, "What have you done? You've deceived me, and you've carried off my daughters like captives in war.* ²⁷ *Why did you run off secretly and deceive me? Why didn't you tell me, so I could send you away with joy and singing to the music of timbrels and harps?* ²⁸ *You didn't even let me kiss my grandchildren and my daughters goodbye. You have done a foolish thing.* ²⁹ *I have the power to harm you; but last night the God of your father said to me, 'Be careful not to say anything to Jacob, either good or bad.'* ³⁰ *Now you have gone off because you longed to return to your father's household. But why did you steal my gods?"*

³¹ *Jacob answered Laban, "I was afraid, because I thought you would take your daughters away from me by force.* ³² *But if you find anyone who has your gods, that person shall not live. In the presence of our relatives, see for yourself whether there is anything of yours here with me; and if so, take it." Now Jacob did not know that Rachel had stolen the gods.*

³³ So Laban went into Jacob's tent and into Leah's tent and into the tent of the two female servants, but he found nothing. After he came out of Leah's tent, he entered Rachel's tent. ³⁴ Now Rachel had taken the household gods and put them inside her camel's saddle and was sitting on them. Laban searched through everything in the tent but found nothing.

³⁵ Rachel said to her father, "Don't be angry, my lord, that I cannot stand up in your presence; I'm having my period." So he searched but could not find the household gods....

...

⁴³ Laban answered Jacob, "The women are my daughters, the children are my children, and the flocks are my flocks. All you see is mine. Yet what can I do today about these daughters of mine, or about the children they have borne? ⁴⁴ Come now, let's make a covenant, you and I, and let it serve as a witness between us."

⁴⁵ So Jacob took a stone and set it up as a pillar. ⁴⁶ He said to his relatives, "Gather some stones." So they took stones and piled them in a heap, and they ate there by the heap. ⁴⁷ Laban called it Jegar Sahadutha, and Jacob called it Galeed.

⁴⁸ Laban said, "This heap is a witness between you and me today." That is why it was called Galeed. ⁴⁹ It was also called Mizpah, because he said, "May the LORD keep watch between you and me when we are away from each other. ⁵⁰ If you mistreat my daughters or if you take any wives besides my daughters, even though no one is with us, remember that God is a witness between you and me."

⁵¹ Laban also said to Jacob, "Here is this heap, and here is this pillar I have set up between you and me. ⁵² This heap is a witness, and this pillar is a witness, that I will not go past this heap to your side to harm you and that you will not go past this heap and pillar to my side to harm me. ⁵³ May the God of Abraham and the God of Nahor, the God of their father, judge between us."

So Jacob took an oath in the name of the Fear of his father Isaac. ⁵⁴ He offered a sacrifice there in the hill country and invited his relatives to a meal. After they had eaten, they spent the night there.

⁵⁵ Early the next morning Laban kissed his grandchildren and his daughters and blessed them. Then he left and returned home.

Genesis 31:22-35, 43-55

Reflect and Respond

The time has come for Jacob and his clan to return to his true home, the promised land pledged to his family by God two generations before. This time the road to Harran will be traveled by more than a man and his camels. When Jacob left home (fleeing from his brother, Esau), he traveled light, but this time he is joined by two wives, two concubines, eleven sons (Benjamin will come later), a daughter, and huge herds of livestock.

When our family goes on vacation, our car seems to be packed for a year, not a week. Traveling with a baby and a toddler means taking all the comforts of home (portable crib, high chair) and all the possible things they might need in any situation. I tend to overpack, since I know that if we forget something important (the favorite stuffed animals are the most important!) we'll be turning around and going back.

Instead of a family vacation, this caravan in Genesis 31 looks more like the circus has come to town. Traveling with tents, children, livestock, and all of their necessities would be a huge undertaking. But Jacob desires to see his home and family again, and so they set out on the long journey.

Read Genesis 31:1-3.

What prompts Jacob's desire to leave?

Laban & his sons were turning against him.

What promise does he receive from God?

To be w/ him

There was one piece of baggage Jacob hadn't counted on. Before they left, Rachel had stolen her father's idols.

Read Genesis 31:19 and 32.

When did Rachel steal the idols?

While Laban was shearing his sheep

Why do you think she did this without telling Jacob?

maybe to claim the family inheritance

According to verse 32, did Jacob know she had taken them?

No, because he said they should die

> *Now Laban had gone to shear his sheep, and Rachel stole her father's household gods. . . . Now Jacob did not know that Rachel had stolen the gods.*
> Genesis 31:19, 32c NRSV

When Abraham left everything he knew behind and followed God's call to go to the promised land, he left not only his family but also their religions of worshiping false gods. Abraham's family was polytheistic, which I describe as having a buffet of gods they could choose from to worship. There were gods for many different occasions and situations: a god of war, a god of the harvest, a

169

god of fertility, a god to control the weather, and so forth. When you wanted to change a certain situation, you prayed and made offerings to the god who had control of that particular domain. The idols representing those gods were clay or wood figures made by human hands.

Read Isaiah 46:5-7. What comparison is made between the One True God and the idols made by human hands?

He creates light & makes darkness
He sends good times & bad times

Although Abraham left behind his family's belief in multiple gods when he pursued God's call and purpose for his life and his family, the family he left behind still worshiped idols, and Laban was part of that family. We're not told if Rachel took the idols with the intention of worshiping them herself, or punishing Laban for his actions toward her or her husband. But we do know that it made Laban furious! Of all the things he could have missed when Jacob snuck away with his daughters, his grandchildren, and much of his flock (though it was a portion of his flock promised to Jacob anyway), he missed his idols the most.

While most in our modern world do not worship clay or wood figurines, the human heart will always be susceptible to idol worship. Laban shows us a clear picture of how we are prone to put idols in our lives, giving them a place of value over our family and over God himself. God is very clear in His desire for us to worship Him alone.

What is the command of Exodus 20:4-5?

You shall not make for yourself an idol

What reason does God give for this command?

punishing children for the iniquity of parents

In God's case, jealousy does not mean that He is vain or needy but simply that He wants us to worship Him alone, because that is the purpose for which we are made.

What are some of the things we tend to put above God as priorities or idols in our lives?

What are one or two things that you, personally, struggle not to place above God in your life?

You shall not make for yourself an idol, whether in the form of anything that is in heaven above, or that is on the earth beneath, or that is in the water under the earth. You shall not bow down to them or worship them; for I the Lord your God am a jealous God, punishing children for the iniquity of parents, to the third and fourth generation of those who reject me.
Exodus 20:4-5
NRSV

The scene of Laban searching Jacob's camp for his idols turns into an amusing one, meant to demean these false gods even further. Jacob has no clue that the idols are in his camp, and he even makes a dangerous vow.

Reread Genesis 31:32. What was Jacob's vow?

If you find anyone who has Laban's gods, killing him.

Jacob might not have made such a rash pledge had he known the idols were in the possession of his beloved wife. But any fear we as readers might have for Rachel's safety is quickly eclipsed by her clever scheme.

What does Rachel tell Laban in Genesis 31:35?

She can't stand up – she's having her period.

The lie Rachel tells Laban may make him wary to search her personal possessions too carefully, but it also humbles those false gods even further because in Jewish understanding a woman's period makes her unclean (Leviticus 15:19). While Christians don't have that belief, the story unfolds in a way that mocks these false gods as something that can be made unclean by human contact, while the One True God can cleanse us from all impurity.

The remainder of the passage is devoted to the parting of the ways of Jacob and Laban. Laban seems to calm down after his strong reaction to Jacob sneaking away with his family and flock, but not before the text gets in one more play on words using Jacob's name as a verb. "You've deceived me," Laban says, or more literally, "you've *Jacobed* me, and you've carried off my daughters like captives in war" (Genesis 31:26). Perhaps they can part friends because they're even now—both grand deceivers having completed one good trick. Although Jacob and Laban have had their differences and, in many ways, have met their conniving match in one another, they reconcile and make a covenant together.

The ability to move past the hurts that other family members have caused us is one that many of us struggle to attain. When we find ourselves the victim of a family member—perhaps not of deception but of betrayal, abuse, or neglect—the scars we carry can mean there is a very real chasm between us and those in our closest circles of family or friendship.

Is there a family member or friend who is estranged from you or others because of a wrong committed in the past? How does that affect your relationship?

What would help you (and/or others) be able to move past the hurt?

The ceremony of reconciliation that Jacob and Laban experienced included a promise not to harm each other further. We can't always count on others to make or fulfill such a promise, and God does not call us to put ourselves in harm's way by placing trust where none is deserved. But God does want us to lift up our hurts and concerns to Him so that He can heal and renew us.

In Laban's last scene in all of Scripture, he does something that reminds us once again of our theme of brokenness and blessing.

What does Laban do in Genesis 31:55?

kissed everyone & went home

Picture the tender scene with Laban blessing his daughters and grandchildren. Laban, of all people, fulfills the job description not only of God but of all God's followers—to bless others.

Rachel and Leah's father blessed them in the end. Unlike Jacob's father, Isaac, Laban didn't withhold that blessing from one or the other child, and he didn't wait until his deathbed to offer it. He gave his blessing freely and plentifully.

Whatever your family story, whatever your experience, I pray that you will not wait to extend a blessing to others. God has blessed you in abundance. He is, even now, planning blessings for you that you have not yet realized. In light of the blessing you have received, make sure you pass the blessing along today and every day.

God has blessed you in abundance. He is, even now, planning blessings for you that you have not yet realized. In light of the blessing you have received, make sure you pass the blessing along today and every day.

Pray About It

God, where there is division or hurt in my family from past experiences, bring healing and hope. Where I have worshiped other things by putting them before You, I ask Your forgiveness. I invite You to take again Your rightful place on the throne of my heart as I give my life in worship in response to Your blessings. Amen.

Act On It

- How is God calling you to extend a blessing to others? Watch and wait for an opportunity to pass along God's blessing to someone today.

Week 5
Video Viewer Guide

Leah had weak eyes; Rachel was lovely. (Genesis 29:16-17)

So Jacob served _____7_____ *years to get Rachel, but they seemed like only a few* __days__ *to him because of his love for her.*

Genesis 29:20 NIV

Jacob requests the wife he has worked and waited for. (Genesis 29:21)

When morning came, there was Leah! So Jacob said to Laban, "What is this you have done to me? I served you for Rachel, didn't I? Why have you __deceived__ *me?"*

Genesis 29:25 NIV

__Competition__ and __comparison__ are toxic elements to our lives and to our families.

Do you not know that your bodies are temples of the Holy Spirit, who is in you, whom you have received from God? You are not your own; you were __bought__ *at a* __price__ .

1 Corinthians 6:19-20 NIV

God loves you simply because you are __His__ .

Week 6
Joseph and His Brothers

The AIDS epidemic leaves behind thousands of new orphans a day on the continent of Africa. Claudine was one of them.

Claudine was five years old when her mother and father died from HIV/AIDS. At five she was left to care for a three-year-old sister and a six-month-old sister. Twenty years ago relatives or neighbors probably would have taken the sisters in, but the sheer number of AIDS orphans has overwhelmed the family systems in Rwanda, and now orphans are often ostracized and ignored.

At first, Claudine went begging to put food in her sisters' stomachs. They found shelter with an elderly blind woman; then a family let them sleep in their cowshed in order to protect the cows from thieves. At age fifteen, Claudine struck up a deal with a landlord where she worked two days a week in exchange for rent. She and her sisters were warm and dry, but on the days she worked for the landlord, they went to bed hungry since she hadn't gone out to beg for food that day. Claudine had to resort to sending her middle sister away to work in another town as a household servant, splitting the family up just to keep everyone fed.

When she heard about a ministry that had come to town to help orphans, Claudine grabbed a large sack on the way to the meeting, assuming she would be receiving food as a handout. To her surprise, they didn't offer food. Instead, they offered so much more: a family, a solution, a new way of life.

Zoe Ministry didn't offer handouts; instead they focused on helping orphans become self-supporting by creating family groups for them. They grouped the orphans into family units of sixty to one hundred children and began empowering the older children to make decisions as leaders of the family while offering grants and training so that they could have a better way than begging to provide for their siblings.

Claudine received two plots of land that Zoe rented for her to raise quick-growing crops. When she grew more than they needed for food, she was able to sell the rest. As she got on her feet, Zoe offered to train her as a seamstress; and then they gave her a sewing machine and the materials she needed to begin a business. She was able to bring her younger sister home, and the reunited family began eating three meals a day for the first time ever.

As a teenager Claudine was a thriving leader in her orphan family group, even giving her testimony at local churches. After some time, though, the other leaders in her group began to notice she looked tired and hungry again. When a concerned representative from Zoe went to the building where she lived to check on her, they found she had adopted six other orphans. Claudine explained that the children had been hungry, so she had invited them home for a meal—and they had stayed. She asked the leader: "How can I speak about what God has done for me and not do the same for others?"

Within Claudine's Zoe orphan family group there was one housing grant given a year, and that year they decided to give it to Claudine and her growing family. They worked together to build her a house where the family could live and thrive together, and they began providing training for others in the household so that they could earn and contribute to the family's needs.

The Christian family around the world reached out in ministry through Zoe to help Claudine. And because of their help, Claudine reached out and made a difference in the lives of other children who became a family together.

As we enter the last major generation in Genesis, we find an important lesson about the contagious nature of grace in families. When one person blesses another, the blessing usually is multiplied. Just like Claudine's family, our Genesis family faced a number of struggles, but God's grace was more contagious than any trouble found on earth.

Day 1: Dream a Little Dream

Read God's Word

¹ *Jacob lived in the land where his father had stayed, the land of Canaan.* ² *This is the account of Jacob's family line.*

Joseph, a young man of seventeen, was tending the flocks with his brothers, the sons of Bilhah and the sons of Zilpah, his father's wives, and he brought their father a bad report about them.

³ *Now Israel loved Joseph more than any of his other sons, because he had been born to him in his old age; and he made an ornate robe for him.* ⁴ *When his brothers saw that their father loved him more than any of them, they hated him and could not speak a kind word to him.*

⁵ *Joseph had a dream, and when he told it to his brothers, they hated him all the more.* ⁶ *He said to them, "Listen to this dream I had:* ⁷ *We were binding sheaves of grain out in the field when suddenly my sheaf rose and stood upright, while your sheaves gathered around mine and bowed down to it."*

⁸ *His brothers said to him, "Do you intend to reign over us? Will you actually rule us?" And they hated him all the more because of his dream and what he had said.*

⁹ *Then he had another dream, and he told it to his brothers. "Listen," he said, "I had another dream, and this time the sun and moon and eleven stars were bowing down to me."*

¹⁰ *When he told his father as well as his brothers, his father rebuked him and said, "What is this dream you had? Will your mother and I and your brothers actually come and bow down to the ground before you?"* ¹¹ *His brothers were jealous of him, but his father kept the matter in mind.*

…

¹⁷ *…So Joseph went after his brothers and found them near Dothan.* ¹⁸ *But they saw him in the distance, and before he reached them, they plotted to kill him.*

¹⁹ *"Here comes that dreamer!" they said to each other.* ²⁰ *"Come now, let's kill him and throw him into one of these cisterns and say that a ferocious animal devoured him. Then we'll see what comes of his dreams."*

²¹ *When Reuben heard this, he tried to rescue him from their hands. "Let's not take his life," he said.* ²² *"Don't shed any blood. Throw him into this cistern here in the wilderness, but don't lay a hand on him." Reuben said this to rescue him from them and take him back to his father.*

²³ *So when Joseph came to his brothers, they stripped him of his robe—the ornate robe he was wearing—* ²⁴ *and they took him and threw him into the cistern. The cistern was empty; there was no water in it.*

^{25} *As they sat down to eat their meal, they looked up and saw a caravan of Ishmaelites coming from Gilead. Their camels were loaded with spices, balm and myrrh, and they were on their way to take them down to Egypt.*

^{26} *Judah said to his brothers, "What will we gain if we kill our brother and cover up his blood? ^{27} Come, let's sell him to the Ishmaelites and not lay our hands on him; after all, he is our brother, our own flesh and blood." His brothers agreed.*

^{28} *So when the Midianite merchants came by, his brothers pulled Joseph up out of the cistern and sold him for twenty shekels of silver to the Ishmaelites, who took him to Egypt.*

^{29} *When Reuben returned to the cistern and saw that Joseph was not there, he tore his clothes. ^{30} He went back to his brothers and said, "The boy isn't there! Where can I turn now?"*

^{31} *Then they got Joseph's robe, slaughtered a goat and dipped the robe in the blood. ^{32} They took the ornate robe back to their father and said, "We found this. Examine it to see whether it is your son's robe."*

^{33} *He recognized it and said, "It is my son's robe! Some ferocious animal has devoured him. Joseph has surely been torn to pieces."*

^{34} *Then Jacob tore his clothes, put on sackcloth and mourned for his son many days. ^{35} All his sons and daughters came to comfort him, but he refused to be comforted. "No," he said, "I will continue to mourn until I join my son in the grave." So his father wept for him.*

Genesis 37:1-11, 17-35

Reflect and Respond

This week we encounter the last major generation of the Genesis family and the dramatic story of Jacob's twelve sons. The story of Jacob's sons takes up the last fourteen chapters of Genesis, a full 28 percent of the book! Why so many chapters for one generation?

For one thing, while other generations focused on the relationship between one or two main characters, this generation has twelve, and their stories are bursting with action-packed material. Another reason we need so many pages to understand their lives is that as our story nears the end, it needs resolution, and right now we're far from it. Generation after generation, the Genesis family has displayed more brokenness than overflowing blessings to those around them. Adam and Eve introduced brokenness into a perfect world; Abraham and Sarah struggled to trust God's promise; Isaac and Rebekah poisoned their family relationships with favoritism; and the most recent generation we've studied with two sets of siblings—Jacob and Esau and Rachel and Leah—was dominated by competition and comparison. How is this family supposed to change the world when the family itself needs so much change? This pivotal generation of Jacob's sons faces the pressure to resolve some of the patterns that have trickled down through the family so that they can become an effective conduit for God's blessings.

In each generation, one member of the family has come to our attention as the main character. In a family of twelve brothers, it will take a strong personality to be noticed and become the leader of a generation. Fortunately, our main character is not lacking in strong personality or in the ability to seek and hold our attention. Young Joseph is the eleventh of twelve brothers and the favorite of his father, Jacob.

Because the favoritism of Jacob's parents had caused such havoc in his family, you might think he would try hard not to make the same mistake with his own boys, especially when he ends up with twelve of them—not to mention a daughter named Dinah. That would be a part of the family script I would think Jacob would gladly tear out and rewrite. Instead, it turns out that Jacob, like his father before him, chooses one son in particular to favor, and that doesn't sit well with his brothers.

In Genesis 37:4, what is the brothers' reaction to their father's favoritism?

hated him & couldn't speak a kind word to him

In the tradition of Cain and Abel, Isaac and Ishmael, and Jacob and Esau, we have a battle of the brothers brewing as the younger brother is favored over the older brothers. If pitting one brother against another caused turmoil in previous generations, showing preference to one brother while multiple older brothers watch causes mayhem even beyond this family's standards.

Joseph's attitude doesn't help his cause. He may be the eventual hero of this story, but in the beginning he's described as a tattletale (Genesis 37:2), a braggart, and a brat. I love that the Bible tells us Joseph's age.

How old is Joseph according to Genesis 37:2?

17

Usually Genesis mentions someone's age only if it has a purpose in the story. So, being familiar with the attitudes of teenagers, we may see the purpose in revealing Joseph's age, perhaps thinking to ourselves, *Well, he's seventeen . . . that explains a lot!*

What two dreams does Joseph describe in Genesis 37:5-9?

p. 176

178

If you were Joseph's brothers, how would you interpret the symbols in his dreams?

How might you feel about this interpretation?

Who rebukes him for the dream in Genesis 37:10? Why?

His father - didn't want to bow down to him

In presenting those dreams, Joseph is either naïve, unwittingly stirring up his brothers' anger toward "daddy's favorite," or intentionally confrontational, rubbing salt in the already raw family wounds. His natural mother, Rachel, died giving birth to the youngest brother, Benjamin. So when Joseph taunts his brothers by describing the sun (their father), moon (their mother), and stars (the brothers themselves) bowing down to him, we know that the moon is Leah, the lifelong rival of his mother, Rachel. That had to stir up all kinds of hurt.

The idea of the eleventh of twelve ruling over his brothers is an idea original to Joseph's dreams. Earlier, a surprising present from his father Jacob had sent exactly the same message.

What did Jacob give to Joseph according to Genesis 37:3?

an ornate robe

The gift was extravagant in more ways than one. For one thing, in a family of all brothers, I'm sure there were a lot of hand-me-downs passed from one to the next. So why did the eleventh son get new (and expensive) clothes? But even more significant, the garment was not just a token of love for the father's favorite; it was a symbol of leadership and succession. Jacob had given Joseph a robe to mark him as heir. In a culture where birth order determines everyone's role and position in a family, this was a shocking declaration.

By choosing Joseph as his heir, Jacob was circumventing the cultural rules about the firstborn (which he obviously never adhered to anyway) and naming the first son of his favorite wife as the next in line to rule the family. This had to be a low blow to the sons of Leah, Zilpah, and Bilhah, making them defensive not only of their own place in the family but also of their mothers, who obviously had been snubbed.

> The garment was not just a token of love for the father's favorite; it was a symbol of leadership and succession.

179

As we saw last week, the trouble between Rachel and Leah might have inspired a law to prevent the same trouble in future generations. Another law found in Deuteronomy 21:15-17 sounds like it was written with Jacob's family in mind. What does it say?

Between their father's preferential treatment and Joseph's dreaming and bragging, the brothers have plenty of reasons to develop a deep hatred for Joseph. It's no wonder that not too far into their story they begin plotting to kill him.

Reread Genesis 37:19-20. What is their plan?

In the midst of their murderous schemes, two brothers come to Joseph's defense. The first is Reuben, who encourages the brothers not to kill him but to throw him in a pit and leave him there. Deciding to do just that, they seize Joseph, confiscate his coat, and roughly toss him into a dried-up cistern. Then they sit down to calmly discuss the matter over lunch. As they do, another brother, Judah, sees a band of traders passing by as an opportunity to suggest that they sell Joseph into slavery. Though harsh treatment, this may be what prevents Joseph's death.

Look back at the chart on page 165. Whose sons are Reuben and Judah? Where do they fall in the birth order?

Reuben's kindness, in particular, is striking. When he returns to the cistern to rescue Joseph—evidently having been absent when they sold Joseph into slavery—he weeps and tears his clothes as a sign of grief. Since Reuben is the eldest of all the brothers, he is the one who should be most threatened by Joseph's potential rise from the bottom of the heap to become the heir. It is Reuben's birthright that is at stake here.

After the brothers slaughter a goat and cover Joseph's coat with its blood, they return together to their father, hand him the bloodstained coat, and say as little as possible about where it came from, letting Jacob draw his own conclusions. Refusing to be comforted, he pledges to mourn for his favorite son until he himself joins him in the grave.

What will happen to our dreamer? Although the dreams God pledged for this family have never been on shakier ground, there is no doubt that God can turn even this situation around. Indeed He loves to find the most hopeless of dreams and help them become a reality.

Joseph's dreams of those around him bowing and scraping have even deeper meaning than anyone in the family may have guessed. He will one day rule over a great number of people and save the lives of many. The potential in this boy dreamer is astonishing, but the road to the fulfilled dream will be a long one.

The trouble with dreams is that sometimes the dreamer isn't ready. In Joseph's case, the dreams are all true. But the dreamer needs work before the dream can be realized. If God had handed Joseph the power and position he desired at this early and immature stage of his life, Joseph probably would not have handled it well. Instead, Joseph will have to wait until he is ready, allowing his character and trust in God to develop through the years.

When God wants us to accomplish big things for His kingdom, He must first prepare in us big character to match big vision.

Can you think of any dreams that God had to prepare you for before entrusting them to you?

What has happened in your life that you wouldn't have been prepared to handle if it had taken place earlier?

God often uses the tool of time to help us grow into His dreams for us. Whatever happens in those years, we can be sure that God will be with us—just as we will see that He was with Joseph.

Pray About It

Lord God, give me big dreams. Help me to see things that I can accomplish for Your kingdom that You have created me uniquely to do. Then give me character to match my vision so that You can trust me with all that I must do. Amen.

> When God wants us to accomplish big things for His kingdom, He must first prepare in us big character to match big vision.

Act On It

- Do you have any dreams that are yet unfulfilled in your life? How might God be preparing you right now for the future that is still to come? Offer your thoughts to God in prayer. In the space below, write an expression of your trust that God will be with you whatever may come between now and the fulfillment of your dream(s).

- What is God calling you to do right now as you wait on your dream(s)?

Day 2: Sudden Changes

Read God's Word

39 [20] *Joseph's master took him and put him in prison, the place where the king's prisoners were confined.*

But while Joseph was there in the prison, [21] *the LORD was with him; he showed him kindness and granted him favor in the eyes of the prison warden.* [22] *So the warden put Joseph in charge of all those held in the prison, and he was made responsible for all that was done there.* [23] *The warden paid no attention to anything under Joseph's care, because the LORD was with Joseph and gave him success in whatever he did.*

40 [1] *Some time later, the cupbearer and the baker of the king of Egypt offended their master, the king of Egypt.* [2] *Pharaoh was angry with his two officials, the chief cupbearer and the chief baker,* [3] *and put them in custody in the house of the captain of the guard, in the same prison where Joseph was confined.* [4] *The captain of the guard assigned them to Joseph, and he attended them.*

After they had been in custody for some time, [5] *each of the two men—the cupbearer and the baker of the king of Egypt, who were being held in prison—had a dream the same night, and each dream had a meaning of its own.*

⁶ *When Joseph came to them the next morning, he saw that they were dejected.* ⁷ *So he asked Pharaoh's officials who were in custody with him in his master's house, "Why do you look so sad today?"*

⁸ *"We both had dreams," they answered, "but there is no one to interpret them."*

Then Joseph said to them, "Do not interpretations belong to God? Tell me your dreams."

⁹ *So the chief cupbearer told Joseph his dream. He said to him, "In my dream I saw a vine in front of me, ¹⁰ and on the vine were three branches. As soon as it budded, it blossomed, and its clusters ripened into grapes. ¹¹ Pharaoh's cup was in my hand, and I took the grapes, squeezed them into Pharaoh's cup and put the cup in his hand."*

¹² *"This is what it means," Joseph said to him. "The three branches are three days. ¹³ Within three days Pharaoh will lift up your head and restore you to your position, and you will put Pharaoh's cup in his hand, just as you used to do when you were his cupbearer. ¹⁴ But when all goes well with you, remember me and show me kindness; mention me to Pharaoh and get me out of this prison. ¹⁵ I was forcibly carried off from the land of the Hebrews, and even here I have done nothing to deserve being put in a dungeon."*

¹⁶ *When the chief baker saw that Joseph had given a favorable interpretation, he said to Joseph, "I too had a dream: On my head were three baskets of bread. ¹⁷ In the top basket were all kinds of baked goods for Pharaoh, but the birds were eating them out of the basket on my head."*

¹⁸ *"This is what it means," Joseph said. "The three baskets are three days. ¹⁹ Within three days Pharaoh will lift off your head and impale your body on a pole. And the birds will eat away your flesh."*

²⁰ *Now the third day was Pharaoh's birthday, and he gave a feast for all his officials. He lifted up the heads of the chief cupbearer and the chief baker in the presence of his officials: ²¹ He restored the chief cupbearer to his position, so that he once again put the cup into Pharaoh's hand— ²² but he impaled the chief baker, just as Joseph had said to them in his interpretation.*

²³ *The chief cupbearer, however, did not remember Joseph; he forgot him.*

Genesis 39:20–40:23

Reflect and Respond

Joseph's station in life has changed in the blink of an eye. Formerly a favored son who was used to the finest clothes in the family, a dinner table overflowing to feed an army of young men, and his father's adoration, he suddenly finds himself a slave. The long journey to Egypt in shackles gives him plenty of time to reflect on the cruelty of his brothers and to wonder how his father is grieving his loss. Joseph faces his own grief over the loss of life as he knew it, the loss of his family, and the death of his dreams. He may have once dreamed of others bowing to him, but the life of a slave means he now will be doing the bowing for the foreseeable future.

This whiplash from the sudden overthrow of his comfortable lifestyle is a good indication of the future Joseph is about to face, since the next few chapters find Joseph hanging on for the roller coaster ride of his life. Just when life knocks him down, Joseph will suddenly rise up. Then just as he begins to get on his feet, we'll suddenly find him flat on his face again. "Suddenly" could become his mantra, since the word is implied around every corner in Joseph's story. His life changes as suddenly as the climate in my home state of Texas, where we like to say: "If you don't like the weather, just wait a minute!"

Slavery is not an enviable station in any culture, but Joseph somehow makes the best of it. He prospers as the second in command to his master Potiphar, and the leadership gifts that came across as pride in his youth now develop into full flower. If we are tempted to question where his accomplishments come from, the Bible is clear about the secret of his success.

Read Genesis 39:2-6. Circle every time the words _Lord_, _blessed_, and _blessing_ are mentioned in this passage. Why does Joseph prosper in slavery?

No sooner have we begun to have some hope that our boy Joseph is going to be okay than suddenly (there's that word again) he's thrown into prison.

Read Genesis 39:7-20. How does Joseph end up in prison?

First defrocked of his precious coat by his brothers, Joseph is now literally stripped of his dignity and reputation by his boss's wife. While doing the right thing may pay off in the long run, Joseph teaches us that the penalty of sin and the reward of virtue are not always immediate. He honors God and his master and finds himself in the slammer.

Once again Joseph lands on his feet. Slave or prisoner, he can bloom where he's planted even in the darkest of dungeons.

Reread Genesis 39:20b-23.

How does Joseph prosper in prison?

How are the attitudes toward Joseph demonstrated by Potiphar and the warden similar?

Twice now Joseph has been victimized—once by his own family with violence, theft, and human trafficking; and now by his employer with sexual harassment, slander, and false imprisonment. What's noteworthy is that he never plays the victim. Throughout the story Joseph shows character and perseverance when most people might have given up.

Unlike his father, Jacob, Joseph does not deceive others or manipulate situations for his own gain. Joseph is honest and hardworking and never lets a tough situation keep him down.

How do the words of Colossians 3:22-25 describe Joseph's attitude?

What can help you to demonstrate character and perseverance despite difficult circumstances?

While in prison, Joseph's inwardly focused gift for dreaming turns outward when he begins to interpret other people's dreams. He befriends two other wrongfully imprisoned servants and interprets their cryptic dreams, one for better and one for worse. Once again he's not afraid to be honest when the dream of one man means that he will be put to death. The other servant returns to Pharaoh's household and forgets about Joseph's service to him until Pharaoh himself experiences a vivid and disturbing dream. Suddenly, the memory of Joseph's gifts is stirred, and Joseph is brought to Pharaoh to see if he can do what all the magicians and wise men of Egypt cannot—decipher the meaning of Pharaoh's dream.

Read Pharaoh's dream and Joseph's interpretation in Genesis 41:17-32. Why do you think it might have been difficult for Joseph to tell the truth about the meaning of Pharaoh's dream? How might his honesty have worked against him in this instance?

Slaves, obey your earthly masters in everything, not only while being watched and in order to please them, but wholeheartedly, fearing the Lord. Whatever your task, put yourselves into it, as done for the Lord and not for your masters, since you know that from the Lord you will receive the inheritance as your reward; you serve the Lord Christ. . . .
Colossians
3:22-25 NRSV

How does Joseph wisely anticipate and avoid a potentially negative response to his interpretation?

Pharaoh's dream means that tough times are ahead for Egypt, and it might not have worked in Joseph's favor to be the bearer of this bad news. So, instead of simply dropping the news of a severe famine in Pharaoh's lap for him to deal with, Joseph also proposes a set of sensible solutions, suggesting that "Pharaoh look for a discerning and wise man and put him in charge of the land of Egypt" to prepare the country for the worst (Genesis 41:33). The power of suggestion works, Pharaoh recognizes the gifts of discernment and leadership in Joseph, and suddenly Joseph goes from convict to cabinet member.

First Potiphar, then the prison warden, and now Pharaoh recognize Joseph's remarkable gifts. Pharaoh is so impressed with Joseph that he elevates him to be his right-hand man. This time Joseph is not running a household or a prison but an empire. Wherever Joseph goes, God blesses him; and when he is blessed, he doesn't hesitate to give credit to God.

How does Joseph give glory to God in each of these situations?

Genesis 39:7-9

Genesis 40:8

Genesis 41:16

Even Pharaoh recognizes where Joseph's remarkable gifts originate, declaring "Can we find anyone like this man, one in whom is the spirit of God?" (Genesis 41:38).

Joseph has been through so many sudden changes, from his comfortable family home to the slave quarters in a strange land, from the pit of a dungeon to second in command of a kingdom. But he doesn't let negative circumstances drive him to despair or success drive him to pride. His resilience makes him levelheaded in the midst of the changes, and his humility drives him to seek God through the good and the bad.

It seems Joseph's character reflects the lessons learned by another prisoner later in Scripture.

Read Philippians 4:11-13.

What lessons does the apostle Paul, who is writing from prison, say that he has learned?

What evidence do you see in Joseph's life to suggest that he has learned these same lessons?

God's blessings are not like a faucet that is turned on in good times and off in bad. God is constantly blessing us, whether our circumstances are favorable or not. God is with us in hard times, but even more than that, God is blessing us at all times. And we can learn to recognize those blessings whether they come to us on a mountaintop of success or in the deep valley of struggle by maintaining an attitude of thankfulness and gratitude.

Joseph is now beginning to see those earlier dreams of leadership and success come true—but not before watching the dreams go down the drain more than once. As we've noted previously, often when God gives us a dream, it takes time for it to unfold. Sometimes, like Joseph, we see our dreams go through distinct phases:

- The birth of the dream
- The death of the dream
- The rebirth or resurrection of the dream

It is never easy to witness the death of a dream, but if we are faithful to see it through to the end, the dream often emerges with God's help in a way that is even better than before.

Have you ever witnessed the death of one of your dreams? If so, describe that experience briefly.

Have you ever seen a new dream emerge that is better than what you had hoped in the beginning? If so, briefly describe what that was like.

> God is constantly blessing us, whether our circumstances are favorable or not. . . . And we can learn to recognize those blessings whether they come to us on a mountaintop of success or in the deep valley of struggle by maintaining an attitude of thankfulness and gratitude.

How is God currently working to bring His dreams into reality in your life?

The hope present throughout Joseph's story is not that God makes the lives of His children easy or carefree but that God is present in our cares and struggles. When the winds of sudden change come, the God of stability and faithfulness stays blessedly the same. I hope that you are finding ways to be faithful to God in your life right now, whether the circumstances that surround you are pleasant or difficult. Like Joseph, your faithfulness can point other people to recognize the presence of an incredible God moving behind the scenes of your life.

> When the winds of sudden change come, the God of stability and faithfulness stays blessedly the same.

Pray About It

God, please help me to be faithful to You in good times and bad. I need Your help not to succumb to a pity party when things are difficult or to become prideful when all is going my way. I want You to be at the center of all things in my life so that, like Joseph, people will recognize that my strength comes from You. Amen.

Act On It

- **How have you seen the faithfulness and blessing of God in the deep valley of struggle? Think of a recent time of struggle, naming it below. Now list the blessings you experienced during that time.**

- **What can you do this week to help others as a way of expressing your gratitude to God for His faithfulness and blessings? Make notes below.**

Day 3: Brotherly Reunion

Read God's Word

¹ When Jacob learned that there was grain in Egypt, he said to his sons, "Why do you just keep looking at each other?" ² He continued, "I have heard that there is grain in Egypt. Go down there and buy some for us, so that we may live and not die."

³ Then ten of Joseph's brothers went down to buy grain from Egypt. ⁴ But Jacob did not send Benjamin, Joseph's brother, with the others, because he was afraid that harm might come to him. ⁵ So Israel's sons were among those who went to buy grain, for there was famine in the land of Canaan also.

⁶ Now Joseph was the governor of the land, the person who sold grain to all its people. So when Joseph's brothers arrived, they bowed down to him with their faces to the ground. ⁷ As soon as Joseph saw his brothers, he recognized them, but he pretended to be a stranger and spoke harshly to them. "Where do you come from?" he asked.

"From the land of Canaan," they replied, "to buy food."

⁸ Although Joseph recognized his brothers, they did not recognize him. ⁹ Then he remembered his dreams about them and said to them, "You are spies! You have come to see where our land is unprotected."…

…

¹⁷ And he put them all in custody for three days.

¹⁸ On the third day, Joseph said to them, "Do this and you will live, for I fear God: ¹⁹ If you are honest men, let one of your brothers stay here in prison, while the rest of you go and take grain back for your starving households. ²⁰ But you must bring your youngest brother to me, so that your words may be verified and that you may not die." This they proceeded to do.

²¹ They said to one another, "Surely we are being punished because of our brother. We saw how distressed he was when he pleaded with us for his life, but we would not listen; that's why this distress has come on us."

²² Reuben replied, "Didn't I tell you not to sin against the boy? But you wouldn't listen! Now we must give an accounting for his blood." ²³ They did not realize that Joseph could understand them, since he was using an interpreter.

²⁴ He turned away from them and began to weep, but then came back and spoke to them again. He had Simeon taken from them and bound before their eyes.

²⁵ Joseph gave orders to fill their bags with grain, to put each man's silver back in his sack, and to give them provisions for their journey. After this was done for them, ²⁶ they loaded their grain on their donkeys and left.

^{27} At the place where they stopped for the night one of them opened his sack to get feed for his donkey, and he saw his silver in the mouth of his sack. ^{28} "My silver has been returned," he said to his brothers. "Here it is in my sack."

Their hearts sank and they turned to each other trembling and said, "What is this that God has done to us?"...

...

^{35} As they were emptying their sacks, there in each man's sack was his pouch of silver! When they and their father saw the money pouches, they were frightened. ^{36} Their father Jacob said to them, "You have deprived me of my children. Joseph is no more and Simeon is no more, and now you want to take Benjamin. Everything is against me!"

^{37} Then Reuben said to his father, "You may put both of my sons to death if I do not bring him back to you. Entrust him to my care, and I will bring him back."

^{38} But Jacob said, "My son will not go down there with you; his brother is dead and he is the only one left. If harm comes to him on the journey you are taking, you will bring my gray head down to the grave in sorrow."

Genesis 42:1-9, 17-28, 35-38

Reflect and Respond

The stories within Genesis could be bound into thematic volumes and distributed to different sections of a bookstore: romance, grief, adventure, relationships. If we stopped Joseph's story at this point, we might assume that it is focused on Joseph as a successful leader, visionary, and gifted manager; and we might place his book in the business section. That book would probably be an instant bestseller: *How to Succeed in Business When Everything Bad Imaginable Happens to You*. Despite all of his challenges, Joseph ends up as second in command to the Pharaoh of an empire. Here is where the book might end, with Joseph at the high point of his career, all of his dreams having come true.

The problem is that Joseph's story is not focused on professional success, and here is the point where it becomes obvious: even after Joseph reaches the highest possible professional success, there still is no resolution to the family conflict with his brothers. The parts of the story that may seem headline-worthy—Joseph's rise to power in Egypt and the international crisis of famine—are really just a backdrop for the more important issue of how this family will find peace with one another after such a tumultuous past. More than a story about international crisis or gifted leadership, this is a story about family. If we ever questioned whether family was important to God, these chapters make it abundantly clear.

If you were to survey the news this week and look at the headlines, what conclusions would you draw about what is important in our culture?

Do you think our culture considers family to be something of great importance? Why or why not?

While the world may have seen the conditions in Egypt as the main story, for us the famine is just the detail that sets into motion the reunion of Joseph's family. The dream that Pharaoh experienced and puzzled over comes true. After seven years of abundance, seven years of great famine hit Egypt and the international community hard. Joseph's role as second in command in the kingdom was an honor before, but now it becomes a matter of life and death as Pharaoh tells all the Egyptians: "Go to Joseph and do what he tells you" (Genesis 41:55). No pressure, right?

Joseph's gifts of foresight, leadership, and the management of Egypt's resources mean that he has the country more than prepared for this difficult time. Not only are Egypt's storehouses well stocked, they begin to provide international aid to the other countries affected, as "all the world came to Egypt to buy grain from Joseph, because the famine was severe everywhere" (Genesis 41:57).

Here is where the story of success and the story of family conflict meet and form one dramatic ending. In the middle of all the refugees heading to Egypt to seek grain for their families is a ragtag group of ten brothers who have traveled far from their home to get enough food to save their family from starvation.

Reread Genesis 42:1-5.

Who initiates the brothers' trip to Egypt? *Jacob*

Which brother does not come with them? Why? *Benjamin because he was afraid hard would come to him*

When the brothers arrive, they don't recognize the powerful man before whom they are forced to beg for grain. Joseph is older now, probably clean-shaven and clothed in the costume and headdress of Egyptian rulers. But Joseph recognizes his brothers immediately. From our point of view as readers, we can see Joseph's emotions fluctuate.

Reread Genesis 42:8-9. What is Joseph's outward reaction?

They were spies

Reread Genesis 42:24. What is Joseph's outward (yet hidden) reaction here?

He cried

It's hard for us to know what is really going on in Joseph's mind during these meetings with his brothers. On the one hand he is emotional, leaving the room to cry so that he doesn't give himself away. On the other hand, his attitude and actions portray him as a harsh, even cruel Egyptian ruler. It seems that Joseph is wrestling with the question of how to handle this family reunion, since the decision between revenge and reconciliation lies completely in his hands. Will there be forgiveness or vengeance in the final act?

The names Joseph has given his two sons reveal how much hurt he still holds onto from the past with his family. According to Genesis 41:50-52, what are their names and what do they mean?

Manasseh – causing to forget
Ephraim – fruitful

While the brothers see only one side of the story, we can see a man who is struggling with confronting his past and what to do with the power he now wields over the brothers who wronged him. For three chapters (42–44) he toys with them like a cat with vulnerable prey, first keeping one brother in prison in Egypt while sending the rest of them home to guarantee he will see them again. Then he sends them home with bags stuffed with grain and the insistence that they return with their younger brother Benjamin. On the way home they realize (with a sinking feeling) that the money they paid for the grain is still in their bags. Joseph repaid the grain fee secretly, but to the brothers it seems they accidentally shoplifted from a very powerful man.

When they must return for more grain (not out of a desire to rescue their imprisoned brother), they know that they have to bring Benjamin as part of the deal. The terrible burden this separation brings to their father reveals how protective the whole family is of Benjamin, the youngest and their father's surviving son from his favorite wife.

Reread Genesis 42:37. What does Reuben promise, and what guarantee does he give?

He can put both of his sons to death if he doesn't bring back Benjamin

The calloused exterior Joseph shows to the brothers is almost exposed when Joseph lays eyes on Benjamin for the first time. Seeing "his own mother's son," for whom he clearly has a fondness, almost puts Joseph over the edge.

Read Genesis 43:29-34.

What blessing does Joseph "blurt out" over Benjamin? (v. 29)

May God be gracious to you, my son

Why does Joseph leave the room? (v. 30)

Overcome w/ emotion

How does he seat his brothers at dinner in a way that no stranger would know? (v. 33)

according to age, oldest to youngest

What special treatment does Benjamin receive at dinner? (v. 34)

He got 5x as much food as the others

In Chapter 44, the tender Joseph gives way again to the angry tyrant. Joseph falsely accuses Benjamin of stealing and insists that he will make Benjamin his slave and force the brothers to return home without him, an act that might kill their father with grief. The brothers who once carelessly tossed Joseph aside without a thought for their father's feelings are beside themselves with concern for Benjamin and for their father's heartache.

If we are able to read this story as if for the first time, not knowing what will happen on the last page, it will be very clear at this point that Joseph's desire for vengeance is winning over his tendency to show compassion or forgiveness. It appears that the one brother he cares for, Benjamin, will remain with him and the others will face an unknown fate.

Joseph's calculated acts of revenge are becoming clear:

- He wrongfully imprisons Simeon just as he was wrongfully imprisoned by Potiphar;
- He falsely accuses the brothers of spying and stealing, just as he was falsely accused by Potiphar's wife;
- And now, in a last act of payback, Joseph is threatening to make Benjamin his slave, just as his brothers cruelly sold him into slavery.

One by one, Joseph is reenacting the wrongs done to him in the cruelty he visits on his brothers. Those reading Joseph's story for the first time have to wonder and worry: what will he do next? Are his brothers' lives in danger?

> One by one, Joseph is reenacting the wrongs done to him in the cruelty he visits on his brothers.

Before we turn the page to tomorrow's reading and the resolution of this story, we have to stop and reflect on the fact that God's children sometimes do terrible things to one another. All of us have probably been wounded either by the carelessness of people we love or even their outright cruelty. God is gentle with our wounds but also gives us guidance on how to handle the wounds inflicted by others.

Read the following Scriptures. How does God call us to respond when we are hurt?

Proverbs 29:21-23

Matthew 5:43-45   *love our enemies*

Matthew 18:21-22

forgive

Have you been hurt by others? Do the wounds you bear still sting even if they were received years ago? Begin with prayer, asking God to help you to repay evil with good and hate with love. Many of us will wrestle, as Joseph did, with how to react to our hurts and those who hurt us even years after the wounds were inflicted. I pray that God will give you the grace to respond not with your own strength but with His.

Pray About It

Lord, my heart bears scars from the neglect and cruelty of others. When I am wronged, teach me how to handle myself as You did on the cross—with compassion toward Your persecutors. When forgiveness is beyond my human strength, give me Your strength and help me to repay evil with good. Amen.

Act On It

- Sometimes the greatest thing we can do for those who have been hurt is to listen to their story. When someone begins telling you a story, put aside your desire to respond with your own story and simply listen, asking questions

---

Then Peter came and said to him, "Lord, if another member of the church sins against me, how often should I forgive? As many as seven times?" Jesus said to him, "Not seven times, but, I tell you, seventy-seven times."
Matthew 18:21-22 NRSV

to clarify. If you know someone who is sick or struggling or has been hurt emotionally, call this person today and say, "What you're going through must be hard. What is that like right now?"

Day 4: Change Agents

Read God's Word

¹ *Then Joseph could no longer control himself before all his attendants, and he cried out, "Have everyone leave my presence!" So there was no one with Joseph when he made himself known to his brothers.* ² *And he wept so loudly that the Egyptians heard him, and Pharaoh's household heard about it.*

³ *Joseph said to his brothers, "I am Joseph! Is my father still living?" But his brothers were not able to answer him, because they were terrified at his presence.*

⁴ *Then Joseph said to his brothers, "Come close to me." When they had done so, he said, "I am your brother Joseph, the one you sold into Egypt!* ⁵ *And now, do not be distressed and do not be angry with yourselves for selling me here, because it was to save lives that God sent me ahead of you.* ⁶ *For two years now there has been famine in the land, and for the next five years there will be no plowing and reaping.* ⁷ *But God sent me ahead of you to preserve for you a remnant on earth and to save your lives by a great deliverance.*

⁸ *"So then, it was not you who sent me here, but God. He made me father to Pharaoh, lord of his entire household and ruler of all Egypt.* ⁹ *Now hurry back to my father and say to him, 'This is what your son Joseph says: God has made me lord of all Egypt. Come down to me; don't delay.* ¹⁰ *You shall live in the region of Goshen and be near me—you, your children and grandchildren, your flocks and herds, and all you have. ...'"*

¹⁴ *Then he threw his arms around his brother Benjamin and wept, and Benjamin embraced him, weeping.* ¹⁵ *And he kissed all his brothers and wept over them. Afterward his brothers talked with him. ...*

...

²⁵ *So they went up out of Egypt and came to their father Jacob in the land of Canaan.* ²⁶ *They told him, "Joseph is still alive! In fact, he is ruler of all Egypt." Jacob was stunned; he did not believe them.* ²⁷ *But when they told him everything Joseph had said to them, and when he saw the carts Joseph had sent to carry him back, the spirit of their father Jacob revived.* ²⁸ *And Israel said, "I'm convinced! My son Joseph is still alive. I will go and see him before I die."*

Genesis 45:1-10, 14-15, 25-28

Reflect and Respond

When God wants to change the world, he starts with a family.

That became clear in our study when we saw that Genesis opened with the story of a family, Adam and Eve—the starting point for both our brokenness and our blessing. God revealed even more of His plan for families when He called Abraham and Sarah to be blessed to be a blessing. Their job was to take the blessings they received from God and magnify them to bless the entire world.

But what happens when the family that is supposed to be a blessing to others is also broken? What happens when they have trouble showing kindness, grace, and compassion even to those within their households, much less spreading that to the world? What will have to happen for our Genesis family to heal from their past turmoil and turn their energy toward blessing one another and the world God has called them to bless? There's only one thing that ever begins that change: when God wants to change a family, He starts with one person.

In this family made up of twelve sons, the hurts have been profound, so the healing must happen—as it does in many of our lives and families—in stages. There are three people who make three profound decisions in the last chapters of this family story, each of them causing a chain reaction that brings reconciliation and healing to the whole family. Let's look at each one together.

Judah: Sacrifice

When we left Joseph yesterday, he was torn between embracing his brothers because of their family connection that bound them together and taking revenge on them for the terrible things he had been through at their hands. For the first-time reader of Genesis, this is a truly suspenseful and heart-pounding moment. Will Joseph take the path of reconciliation or revenge? Will he follow the fraternal example of Cain and Abel? Or can God turn his heart despite the damage that has been done?

The moment that changes Joseph's heart is possible because of the actions of one of his brothers, Judah. When the brothers last left their father behind in Canaan, they had to beg to bring the youngest, Benjamin, with them. Joseph, in the guise of the tough Egyptian ruler, had demanded that they bring Benjamin when they return, even holding Simeon hostage in prison until they were all together again.

Read Genesis 43:8-10. What did Judah promise their father so that he would let Benjamin go with them?

When God wants to change a family, He starts with one person.

Instead of placating Joseph, Benjamin's presence in Egypt causes Joseph to set into motion a new plot. He falsely accuses Benjamin of stealing a prized and valuable silver cup and then declares that he will keep Benjamin as his slave. The brothers are beside themselves, knowing that their father will be overwhelmed with grief. Suddenly, Judah shocks them all by proposing a revolutionary solution.

What is Judah's surprising proposal in Genesis 44:33-34?

All of the brothers are panicking over the possible loss of Benjamin. All of them are anticipating the grief of returning home without him, having lost yet another brother, the youngest and now favorite son of their father. But Judah alone is willing to trade places with Benjamin, to sacrifice his life and his future so that Benjamin will have a future and their father will be spared the immense grief all the brothers are dreading. Judah alone knows the power of sacrifice. This single act melts Joseph's heart and allows healing to begin in the family.

Sacrifice moves people. Sacrifice jolts us out of our daily routine of putting "me first" and makes us wonder: *Why would you go out of your way for me? What could possibly motivate you to put my interests before your own?*

Judah's act of sacrifice changed the course for this family, just as the selfless acts of many people before him and since have shaped families to be places where we learn to care for others with generous hearts.

Has someone ever melted your heart by putting your needs first or by performing an act of sacrifice that was unexpected and undeserved? If so, briefly describe what happened.

The family calling that God gave to Abraham and Sarah predicted that they would be "blessed to be a blessing" to all the nations. In one respect, Joseph's position in Egypt fulfills that prediction because Egypt and the surrounding nations are blessed by Joseph's foresight and leadership. But the larger blessing comes when God sends His own Son, Jesus, to be born into this family and His sacrifice brings the greatest blessing the world has ever known.

Jesus is born with a pedigree of sacrifice. According to Revelation 5:4-5, which of the twelve brothers in this family is Jesus' direct ancestor?

> Sacrifice moves people. Sacrifice jolts us out of our daily routine of putting "me first" and makes us wonder: *Why would you go out of your way for me?*

197

Jesus is born into the tribe of Judah. The lineage of sacrifice that turned the tide for Joseph's family would bring the ultimate sacrifice that would bring blessing to all people.

Joseph: Changing Course

The moment Joseph hears Judah pledge to give his life and serve as a slave in exchange for their younger brother's freedom, Joseph's cruel façade breaks down. He sends all the Egyptians out of the room, comes down from his place of authority to approach his brothers, and reveals his identity. They are immediately horrified and afraid for their lives, knowing the punishment they deserve and Joseph's power over them. But he reassures them that his attitude toward them is one of forgiveness.

While past generations of the family (Cain and Abel, Isaac and Ishmael, Rachel and Leah) showed no signs of reconciliation, Joseph finds the courage to pursue a path of peace for the future of this family. For generations this family has lived with a script of competition and revenge. Their father Jacob and his brother, Esau, had an encounter of forgiveness, but we have no record of their relationship after that moment to know if the relationship was restored. Joseph chooses a new path, unlike his ancestors, to forgive his brothers and live in peace with them.

Describe the scene in Genesis 45:14-15.

Joseph is the family member who breaks the family cycle and begins a new way of relating within the family. Whatever cycles have played out in your family in the past, you were not meant to stay in an ongoing cycle of defeat. God calls us to be new creations, to chart a new course as the first generation that chooses a new path.

Read 2 Corinthians 5:16-20. As a new creation in Christ, how can you offer the message of reconciliation—for others to be reconciled to God and to one another?

When Joseph's brothers fear his retribution for their cruel actions in the past, he reassures them that although they meant to do him harm, he has seen God's hand at work even in the toughest of situations. He reiterates this later in the last chapter of Genesis with this famous verse: "You intended to harm me, but God intended it for good to accomplish what is now being done, the saving of many lives" (Genesis 50:20).

> Whatever cycles have played out in your family in the past, you were not meant to stay in an ongoing cycle of defeat. God calls us to be new creations, to chart a new course as the first generation that chooses a new path.

What the brothers intended for harm, God used for good. God's blessings are so great that they have overwhelmed the evil, the brokenness, the struggle of this family and the world they live in.

Whatever struggles we see, God's blessings are always at work behind the scenes, taking what was meant for harm and bringing God's goodness in the end. Although this is hard to see in the present, the hindsight of eternity will someday help us see with God's vision what we cannot see with our human eyes.

Have you ever been able to look back and see how God's blessing was at work in your life during difficult times? If so, when?

Why do you think this is easier to do in retrospect than when you're in the midst of struggles?

Jacob: Abundant Blessing

So far we've seen drastic changes in Jacob's family, beginning with Judah, who put aside selfishness for sacrifice, and continuing with Joseph, who chose the pathway to peace and reconciliation, charting a new course for their family's future.

The Book of Genesis closes with these brothers living together in Egypt in a pocket of peace and prosperity—despite the want and famine going on around them. At the close of the book, their father, Jacob, knows that he is in his last days. When the time comes for him to give a blessing to his son and heir, he must be reflecting on what happened when his own father was in the same situation. Isaac had felt that he had only one blessing to give, and so when Jacob stole that blessing, there was none left for Esau. So for Jacob's last scene, he chooses to do something different.

Read Genesis 49:1. Whom does Jacob call to his bedside?

Then Jacob called his sons, and said: "Gather around, that I may tell you what will happen to you in days to come."
Genesis 49:1
NRSV

Instead of summoning just one favorite son as his father had, Jacob calls all of his boys around him. The tender scene told in Genesis 49 is one of family togetherness made possible only because of God's overwhelming blessing that already has changed the course of their family.

Instead of speaking to only one son, Jacob gives a blessing to every one of his twelve sons. What a difference from the previous generation! Granted, some of the sons have a checkered past and a questionable future, and so some of the blessings are more challenging than others. But Jacob, known as Israel since his wrestling bout with God, places his hand on each of his twelve sons, speaks words about their future, and acknowledges that they are unique and special individuals. Instead of a situation of scarcity where there aren't enough blessings to go around, on his deathbed Jacob emulates God's abundance. God's abundant blessings have flowed into this family, and now they overflow from Israel to his sons—and from there to the twelve tribes that they will become.

When God wants to change the world, he starts with a family.
When God wants to change a family, he starts with one person.

How are you called to be the person who brings hope and peace to your generation? I hope that you have become aware of God's abundant blessings in your own life. Like Jacob, God has more than enough blessing to go around. He is always abundantly bringing goodness and mercy to His children. You are lavishly loved by your Father. You are blessed by His hand so that those blessings can overflow. You are blessed to be a blessing.

> God has more than enough blessing to go around. He is always abundantly bringing goodness and mercy to His children.

Pray About It

Father God, help me to see the ways You want to use me to bring reconciliation, peace, and abundance to my own family and to the world. Thank You for those who have gone before me and brought changes so that I can live a life of joy. Help me to be a change agent to bring blessing to my family and to the world. Amen.

Act On It

- **On a separate piece of paper, draw a family tree, going as far back as you can from immediate memory. (If you did the group activity during your Week 2 session, you may want to refer to the family tree you made.) Using memories or stories you've heard, write a description next to people who have brought blessings that have trickled down through the generations. Next to your own name, write some words describing the blessings you believe you bring to your family. Make some notes below to get started.**

Day 5: Our New Family

Read God's Word

¹ *Some time later Joseph was told, "Your father is ill." So he took his two sons Manasseh and Ephraim along with him.* ² *When Jacob was told, "Your son Joseph has come to you," Israel rallied his strength and sat up on the bed.*

³ *Jacob said to Joseph, "God Almighty appeared to me at Luz in the land of Canaan, and there he blessed me* ⁴ *and said to me, 'I am going to make you fruitful and increase your numbers. I will make you a community of peoples, and I will give this land as an everlasting possession to your descendants after you.'*

⁵ *"Now then, your two sons born to you in Egypt before I came to you here will be reckoned as mine; Ephraim and Manasseh will be mine, just as Reuben and Simeon are mine.* ⁶ *Any children born to you after them will be yours; in the territory they inherit they will be reckoned under the names of their brothers.* ⁷ *As I was returning from Paddan, to my sorrow Rachel died in the land of Canaan while we were still on the way, a little distance from Ephrath. So I buried her there beside the road to Ephrath"* (that is, Bethlehem).

⁸ *When Israel saw the sons of Joseph, he asked, "Who are these?"*

⁹ *"They are the sons God has given me here," Joseph said to his father.*

Then Israel said, "Bring them to me so I may bless them."

¹⁰ *Now Israel's eyes were failing because of old age, and he could hardly see. So Joseph brought his sons close to him, and his father kissed them and embraced them.*

¹¹ *Israel said to Joseph, "I never expected to see your face again, and now God has allowed me to see your children too."*

¹² *Then Joseph removed them from Israel's knees and bowed down with his face to the ground.* ¹³ *And Joseph took both of them, Ephraim on his right toward Israel's left hand and Manasseh on his left toward Israel's right hand, and brought them close to him.* ¹⁴ *But Israel reached out his right hand and put it on Ephraim's head, though he was the younger, and crossing his arms, he put his left hand on Manasseh's head, even though Manasseh was the firstborn.*

¹⁵ *Then he blessed Joseph and said,*

"May the God before whom my fathers
     Abraham and Isaac walked faithfully,
the God who has been my shepherd
     all my life to this day,
¹⁶ *the Angel who has delivered me from all harm*
     —may he bless these boys.

May they be called by my name
      and the names of my fathers Abraham and Isaac,
and may they increase greatly
      on the earth."

[17] *When Joseph saw his father placing his right hand on Ephraim's head he was displeased; so he took hold of his father's hand to move it from Ephraim's head to Manasseh's head.* [18] *Joseph said to him, "No, my father, this one is the firstborn; put your right hand on his head."*
    [19] *But his father refused and said, "I know, my son, I know. He too will become a people, and he too will become great. Nevertheless, his younger brother will be greater than he, and his descendants will become a group of nations."* [20] *He blessed them that day and said,*

"In your name will Israel pronounce this blessing:
    'May God make you like Ephraim and Manasseh.'"

So he put Ephraim ahead of Manasseh.

Genesis 48:1-20

Reflect and Respond

Each week during their Friday evening Sabbath celebration, Jewish families offer a blessing to their daughters and sons. For a daughter, they place a hand on her head and offer the words: "May God make you like Sarah, Rebecca, Rachel, and Leah." For a son, they place a hand on his head and bless him with the words: "May God make you like Ephraim and Manasseh." This powerful tie to the family stories of the past helps children realize that they are loved and blessed and part of a larger family dating all the way back to Genesis.[1]

Why Ephraim and Manasseh? Why not ask God to make them like Abraham? Or Jacob? Or Joseph? These two sons of Joseph were born in Egypt to an Egyptian mother. Their grandfather Jacob (or Israel) requested that Joseph bring these two sons to his deathbed so that he might bless them.

What touching statement does Jacob make to his favored son Joseph in Genesis 48:11 about Joseph and his offspring?

When they arrive, Jacob declares his intentions: he wants to adopt the two boys. Instead of being his grandsons, they will be considered his sons, part of the famed twelve tribes of Israel who will inherit the promised land. Although the final blessing Jacob offers is with his hands on the heads of the two boys, the Bible clearly says this is a blessing for someone else.

According to Genesis 48:15, who is Jacob blessing?

Jacob is blessing Joseph by blessing his sons. Loving parents understand what a joy and blessing it is when their children are happy and at peace. For Jacob to pass on a blessing to Joseph's sons is the best gift Joseph could receive.

What are some of the blessings you wish for your children or for the young people in your family or community of faith?

This touching family scene is a picture of healing and restoration in a family. Jacob, who spent his childhood trying to grab things away from family members, has matured so much that he wants to pass blessings on to others. Joseph, who in his young adult years bragged that he would be the greatest in his family, enjoys witnessing the blessing of his sons. In the future when the twelve tribes of Israel are listed, Joseph's name is often not among them. Instead, Ephraim and Manasseh take his place (see Numbers 2). Joseph has discovered what the apostle Paul will write later, that among all the gifts God can bestow, the greatest of them all is love (1 Corinthians 13:13).

The scene of full adoption into God's chosen family is quite an honor for Ephraim and Manasseh, who might have been considered second-class citizens with their Egyptian birth and upbringing. Instead, Jacob lifts them up as his own sons, central and important to the bright future of their family in the land God has given them.

When we read this story of adoption, it teaches us something about another adoption that the Bible will introduce years later. The adoption is our own. Because of what God has done through His Son, Jesus, you and I have been welcomed into this amazing family.

Read Galatians 3:7-9. What is the requirement for being called a child of Abraham? (v. 7)

Instead of only those who are blood-related to Abraham, Isaac, and Jacob bearing the title of "God's chosen people," now those who trust in the name of Jesus are welcomed with the same open arms into God's family.

Read Galatians 4:4-7.

According to verse 5, what do we receive?

What are the two titles we are given in verse 7?

Jacob said, "May God make you like Ephraim and Manasseh" (Genesis 48:20). They were adopted as full heirs of Jacob. We are adopted as full heirs through Christ, not because of anything we have done, but because of God's gracious love for us. Because of Jacob's love for his son Joseph, Jacob adopted Joseph's sons as his own. Because of God's love for His Son, Jesus, and because of Jesus' sacrifice on the cross, we are now fully adopted as part of God's family.

While Galatians uses the metaphor of adoption, the Book of Romans uses another metaphor.

How does Romans 11:17-18 describe our adoption into God's family?

These verses talk about an olive tree that has a new branch grafted into it. In the practice of horticulture, a tree may be carefully cut in a certain place and a branch from another tree inserted into that cut so that it begins to grow as its own branch. Here is the picture of a family tree with branches that have been grafted in through the wounds that Christ received on the cross. While we may have entered the family by ways that are different than our ancestors Abraham, Isaac, Jacob, and Joseph—who were born into the family—we are still thriving and growing branches of the family tree, nurtured by our roots in Christ.

When Jacob blesses Ephraim and Manasseh and adopts them as his own, he does so in an unconventional manner. When his own father, Isaac, gave his final blessing, Jacob tricked him into giving the blessing meant for the older son, Esau, to him. Now, as Jacob reaches out to bless the two grandsons (now adopted sons), he mirrors that scene—not as a mistake but as an intentional decision.

In Genesis 48:14 and 17-19, what does Jacob do as he is blessing the boys?

> Because of God's love for His Son, Jesus, and because of Jesus' sacrifice on the cross, we are now fully adopted as part of God's family.

Once again in this family the younger child is blessed over the older. This is a sign of God's unconventional desire to spread His love to everyone, even those that the culture would not expect to be worthy of great blessing.

Read Galatians 3:26-29. Who does the apostle Paul say are children of God, and how is this possible?

Those who have been considered "second class" have been given a place in the family too. Younger and older, slave and free, male and female, Jew and Gentile—any who are adopted by Christ are heirs to the greatest fortune imaginable.

We've learned that Abraham's family is our family. I hope you will see yourself as part of this family, invited in by God because He considers you worthy in Christ. This is an amazing heritage. We have our moments of brokenness, but they are far overshadowed by God's continual blessings. This family is blessed in so many ways. I'm glad that together we can call it our own.

You are His. You are loved. You are blessed.

Pray About It

Father God, thank You for adopting me as Your child. Thank You for the amazing inheritance I have in Jesus Christ. Help me to see myself as You see me, a child worthy of Your great blessings no matter what status I've been given by the world. Thank You for making me part of this amazing family of faith. Amen.

Act On It

- **You are part of the worldwide family of faith! Think of some ways families care for one another. Then describe below how you can support your family of faith locally and globally in similar ways.**

Week 6
Video Viewer Guide

When God wants to change the world, He starts with a ___family___.

When God wants to change a family, He starts with one ___person___.

Nothing can separate us from God. (Romans 8:38-39)

For I am convinced that ___5th graders___ cannot separate me from the love of God that is in Christ Jesus.

50/20 Vision:

"As for you, you meant ___evil___ *against me; but God meant it for* ___good___ *."*

Genesis 50:20 NKJV

Joseph had the power to be a transforming force in his ___family___

so that his family would be a transforming force in the ___world___.

God blessed him, so he would be a blessing.

Notes

Week 1

1. "Genesis," http://dictionary.reference.com/browse/genesis.
2. "Bereshit," http://www.hebrew4christians.com/Scripture/Parashah/Summaries/Bereshit/bereshit.html.
3. "Elohim," http://www.blueletterbible.org/lang/lexicon/lexicon.cfm?strongs=H430&t=KJV.
4. "Ruakh," http://www.blueletterbible.org/lang/lexicon/lexicon.cfm?strongs=H7307&t=KJV.
5. Leon R. Kass, *The Beginning of Wisdom* (Chicago: University of Chicago Press, 2003), p. 37.
6. "Tselem," http://biblesuite.com/hebrew/6754.htm.
7. "Yatsar," http://biblesuite.com/hebrew/3335.htm.
8. "Adamah," http://biblesuite.com/hebrew/127.htm.
9. "Adam," http://biblesuite.com/hebrew/120.htm.
10. "Ezer," http://www.blueletterbible.org/lang/lexicon/lexicon.cfm?strongs=H5828.
11. Walter Brueggeman, *Genesis*, Interpretation (Atlanta: Westminster John Knox, 1982), p. 34.
12. Mary Phiper, *The Shleter of Each Other* (New York: Ballantine Books, 1996), p. 137.

Week 3

1. "Typology" in *The Dictionary of Jesus and the Gospels*, ed. Joel Green, Scot McKnight, and Howard Marshall (Downers Grove, IL: Intervarsity Press, 1992), p. 862.
2. Gerhard von Rand, *Genesis: A Commentary* (Philadelphia: Westminster Press, 1972), p. 254.
3. "Eliezer," http://biblesuite.com/hebrew/461.htm.
4. "Eliezer," http://www.babycenter.com/baby-names-eliezer-480475.htm.

5. "Elohim," http://www.blueletterbible.org/lang/lexicon/lexicon.cfm?strongs=H430&t=KJV.
6. "Ezer," http://biblesuite.com/hebrew/5828.htm.
7. Keith Krell, "The Fingerprints of God," https://bible.org/seriespage/fingerprints-god-genesis-241-67.
8. Victor Hamilton, *Genesis*, NICOT 1 (Grand Rapids: Eerdmans, 1990), p.
9. Ibid., p. 11.

Week 4

1. Theodore Roosevelt, http://www.goodreads.com/quotes/696198-comparison-is-the-thief-of-joy.
2. Victor Hamilton, *Genesis*, NICOT 1 (Grand Rapids: Eerdmans, 1990), p. 182.
3. Ibid., p. 185.
4. Walter Brueggeman, *Genesis*, Interpretation (Atlanta: Westminster John Knox, 1982), p. 227.
5. Although all of these observations can be made in a close, side-by-side reading of the story of Jacob and Esau and the story of the Prodigal Son, I am indebted to a book by Kenneth Bailey called *Jacob and the Prodigal* (Downers Grove, IL: Intervarsity, 2003) for bringing many of them to my attention.
6. Kenneth Bailey, *The Cross and the Prodigal* (Downers Grove, IL: Intervarsity, 2005), p. 41.

Week 5

1. PR Newswire, "The Evolution of Dating," http://www.prnewswire.com/news-releases/the-evolution-of-dating-matchcom-and-chadwick-martin-bailey-behavioral-studies-uncover-a-fundamental-shift-in-how-people-meet-91608029.html.
2. Victor Hamilton, *Genesis*, NICOT 1 (Grand Rapids: Eerdmans, 1990), p. 253.
3. Leon Kass, *The Beginning of Wisdom* (Chicago: University of Chicago Press, 2003), p. 423.
4. Ibid.
5. Hamilton, p. 255.
6. "Bekor," http://biblesuite.com/hebrew/1060.htm.

Week 6

1. http://www.jtsa.edu/prebuilt/ParashahArchives/5761/vayehi.shtml.